THE ABM PLAYBOOK FOR B2B MARKETING

with 60+ Tactics

SAI KRISHNA YALLAPU

notionpress.com

INDIA · SINGAPORE · MALAYSIA

Copyright © Sai Krishna Yallapu 2023
All Rights Reserved.

ISBN 979-8-89066-825-7

This book has been published with all efforts taken to make the material error-free after the consent of the author. However, the author and the publisher do not assume and hereby disclaim any liability to any party for any loss, damage, or disruption caused by errors or omissions, whether such errors or omissions result from negligence, accident, or any other cause.

While every effort has been made to avoid any mistake or omission, this publication is being sold on the condition and understanding that neither the author nor the publishers or printers would be liable in any manner to any person by reason of any mistake or omission in this publication or for any action taken or omitted to be taken or advice rendered or accepted on the basis of this work. For any defect in printing or binding the publishers will be liable only to replace the defective copy by another copy of this work then available.

Praise for *The ABM Playbook for B2B Marketing*

"The way Sai has simplified ABM is just fantastic. It's a straightforward book to read but a very powerful practical guide with many implementation ideas. I recommend this book to every marketer who wants to take their ABM skills to a new level of impact and experience. I am personally going to consume some of these ideas for my own business campaigns."

–Sanjeev Aggarwal,
Global Head, BFSI CMO Initiative, TCS.

"The ABM Playbook for B2B Marketing" is an invaluable resource for marketers seeking to understand and implement ABM strategies. With its clear explanations, practical examples, and comprehensive coverage of key topics, the book equips readers with the knowledge and tools necessary to develop effective ABM programs. Whether you are new to ABM or looking to enhance your existing strategies, this book serves as an essential guide."

–Sudhanshu Tripathi,
Head Marketing & Growth, Quick Heal.

"Very detailed and well-documented handbook for a B2B business development team. The different techniques and multiple use cases are making it extremely easy to understand and implement. A complete science had been put behind ABM and have created well-researched processes around it."

–Shalini Sankar,
National Head-Business Development,
Laqshya Media Group.

"This book on Account-based Marketing (ABM) could not have come at a better time, as interest and adoption of ABM are rapidly increasing. With over 60 practical tactics, this book provides a wealth of creative ideas and strategies for both experienced and beginner marketers."

–Arun Gopalaswami,
CEO & Cofounder, Recotap.

"A comprehensive guide to jump-starting your ABM program. Well-written, clear, and concise, the book is a must-read for anyone who is getting into account-based marketing and can quickly scale up and run comprehensive programs based on the detailed tactics included in this book. This book doesn't just speak about strategies, but also guides on how to adopt, implement and get results from your ABM program."

–Karthik Shankar,
Marketing Lead of a Fortune 500 Company.

"This book provides an exceptional roadmap for navigating the complex landscape of Account-Based Marketing, empowering professionals to unlock new levels of success in their campaigns. With insightful strategies, practical advice, and real-world examples, this book equips B2B marketers with the tools they need to drive meaningful engagements, build lasting relationships, and generate remarkable ROI. A must-read for anyone serious about achieving growth in the digital age."

–Kawalpreet Singh,
Sr.Director, Marketing & Communications, JLL India.

"Saikrishna Yallapu has packed into his insightful book on Account-based Marketing (ABM), years of passion and experience in Marketing, specially in the context of B2B Marketing. The book has been very creatively brought out, making it unputdownable. His 61 tactics for ABM are indeed very practical for anyone to adopt. Mapping the tactics to top, middle and end of the marketing funnel is indeed a unique approach. Given the rapid advances in technology-enabled marketing, his mapping the material presented to different ways of marketing makes the book very contemporary. If you have anything to do with ABM, I would strongly recommend that you internalise the lessons contained in this book."

–DVR Seshadri,
Professor of Practice in the Marketing area,
ISB, Hyderabad.

"This book provides a solid foundation of ABM concepts, and careful selection of tactics that you can leverage, given the nature and maturity of your business. An ABM approach needs to evolve as the business expands in terms of portfolio, geographic extent and mix of customers - because of which your ABM marketing mix can never be static. Hence the art is to balance the discipline of the teams to commit to the agreed ABM approach, while having enough agility to evolve with changing times and organizational context - for which this book provides all the necessary tools and practical examples."

–Anurag Garg,
Chief Strategy & Marketing Officer, Thales.

"SaiKrishna Yallapu's book is a whiff of fresh air in the plethora of books that hit the marketing domain every year. In an era of digital marketing and a digital economy, ABM Playbook is a tool / Resource to get results. With 60 plus techniques, tools and advice on how to get output this marketing and business book is a must read and reference for all marketers, digital owners, digital transformation catalysts, CDOs, CIOs and anyone who wishes to build a brand and business. Sai's insights as a practitioner are akin to a master chef who actually shows you how to cook the perfect dish. Sai is India's Seth Godin in the making. A must read for students and practitioners of marketing. I am sure Sai's book will sell a million copies very soon."

–Dr. Annurag Batra,
Serial Entrepreneur, Angel Investor, Author,
TV Show host, Member of the Board of Governors of MDI,
Chairman BW Businessworld and Founder exchange4media.

"This book clearly identifies the key milestones of an ABM landscape and defines what each milestone means and what it takes to successfully carve this journey. The narrative is succinct without being too verbose and engages the reader to build their interest on the topic of ABM and once they get to understand it, they will have a comprehensive list of ABM tactics with clear steps to execute them with relevant examples and business cases."

–Sayeed S,
Integrated Marketing, Account Based Marketing, Ex-Deloitte.

"ABM, or Account-Based Marketing, has undeniably become one of the most buzzworthy 3 lettered terms in the past few years, right alongside GPT. As CMOs and CROs eagerly embrace ABM, hoping it will serve as the ultimate solution for their lead and revenue generation challenges, others perceive it as a costly and labor-intensive software-driven endeavor.

In light of this prevailing landscape, I am thrilled to introduce Sai's forthcoming book on ABM. This playbook couldn't come at a more opportune time, offering invaluable insights into the core concepts and fundamentals of ABM in a remarkably clear and concise manner. Whether you are a seasoned revenue marketer or just starting your journey, this playbook will equip you with readily applicable strategies and techniques.

Collaborating with Sai on the ideation and creation of this playbook has been an absolute pleasure. Sai's extensive experience as a practitioner, coupled with his creative thinking, shines through the pages. His deep understanding of the intricacies of ABM and his ability to distill complex ideas into practical guidance make this book an indispensable resource.

Within the following chapters, Sai deftly navigates the ABM landscape, unravelling its intricacies while demystifying the common misconceptions surrounding it. With each turn of the page, readers will find themselves empowered with actionable knowledge that can be immediately implemented within their own organizations.

Whether you are seeking a comprehensive introduction to ABM or looking to refine your existing strategies, Sai's Playbook on ABM is a must-read. I am confident that you will find immense value in the expertise shared within these pages, and I applaud Sai for his dedication to empowering marketers with the knowledge they need to thrive in today's rapidly evolving business landscape."

–Amit Shah
SVP - CMO & Head
Global Business Development, Zycus.

This book will be helpful for new and existing businesses. A number of strategies are given on how to handle business on an account basis.

Use and act.

Contents

Why should you buy this book?

➢ **Do you have a friend** who is studying MBA or working as a Marketer?

You can gift this book to your friend who is a Marketer or aspiring to be a Marketer.

➢ **Are you an entrepreneur or heading a revenue team?**

You can get this book for your marketing or sales or account management team.

➢ **Are you a Marketer?**

You can buy this book for the passionate marketer in you.

How to use this book

```
if (you == ABM Expert)

{

    Start from(Chapter:"60+ ABM Tactics");

}

else

{

    Start from(this.page)

}
```

You can use this book as a handbook for referring directly to the tactics. Use the Glossary section to find out the tactics you need based on the stage of the funnel and channel you want.

About the Author

Sai Krishna Yallapu

Sai Krishna Yallapu is a passionate marketing professional with over 15 years of experience. He is specialized in Account-Based Marketing (ABM) and Brand Positioning. Sai Krishna has been instrumental in helping organizations of various sizes and industries to transform their businesses into brands and brands into iconic brands.

With a deep passion for understanding customer needs and delivering targeted marketing solutions, Sai Krishna has become a recognized expert in the field of ABM. He is keen on understanding the evolving marketing landscape and stays at the forefront of industry trends and best practices.

In addition to his expertise in ABM, Sai Krishna is also an influential figure in the digital marketing community. He runs a YouTube channel called "InLoveWithMarketing," where he shares valuable insights, practical tips, and in-depth discussions on various marketing topics, including ABM strategies, digital marketing trends, customer engagement, and more.

Sai Krishna continues to contribute to the world of marketing, help professionals and organizations achieve their marketing goals and drive business success.

LinkedIn: Saikrishnality

Youtube: InLoveWithMarketing

Email: Saikrishnality@gmail.com 

Foreword

The ABM Playbook for B2B Marketing is a well-crafted handy, crisp and highly effective handbook for all the b2b software/IT segment marketers who are involved in demand generation through ABM. Sai Krishna, the author brings in his passion, intense commitment and much appreciated trait of sharing the knowledge of his with the community. The book is an ideal reference guide that can be handy at all times of the ABM life cycle.

Whether you are a b2b SaaS or b2b IT services marketer this book serves ready reckoner. The beauty of the book is, it's an apt reflection of a hands-on approach with deep reflections of simple, yet very effective experiences and tips that the author has himself explored, implemented and measured. The handbook not only explains ABM in simple terms, but takes you through every journey map across the demand funnel and provides actionable techniques for every stage of the funnel. Towards the end, the author also outlines the challenges every ABM professional has to encounter which again are an outcome of what the author has personally experienced, navigated and solved.

The metrics to measure the outcomes and the success, progress being achieved at all stages is a great effort that the author has put in. Finally, this book is just not for the marketers alone as the author rightly emphasizes. ABM is an art and a science that has to be collectively practiced by teams across Sales, Product, Customer Success, Delivery/ Engineering and of course Marketing.

The book's notion to put customer at the center of everything that ABM does is the most important asset that a marketer can carry into every day's work. The book is so nicely written that you can just pick up a technique depending on the stage of ABM you are in and see it for yourself.

Go and have a copy of the book and trust me you would not be disappointed. You will feel energized, motivated and enthused to practice the art of ABM with desirable outcomes that can be achieved, measured and progressed upon using the tactics given.

Good job Sai Krishna and I truly have seen the hours and countless nights you have put in to put together this book. I am sure your zeal to learn, share, co-create and build this art of ABM is going to be an inspiration, force multiplier for many more marketers. It's a jumpstart kit, it's a steroid and booster for marketers to accelerate their ABM journeys. I look forward to more such works from you Sai Krishna and I thank you for giving me an opportunity to review your book and also be a little part of this journey.

As they say, you have just begun and the best is yet to come. Keep writing and Keep Sharing. Here is for all the marketers.

Cheers,
Sairam Vedam,
CMO, Cigniti Technologies,
BBC Knowledge Series, CMO Asia and World Marketing Congress, Enterprise IT Awarded Global Marketing Leader, Forbes Published Marketing and Branding Thought Leader, Blogger, Teacher and a Lifelong student.

Thank you!

I thank the reader, __________________________________ (please write your name here) for choosing to pick up the knowledge in this book.

I thank **Sairam Vedam** and **Subhendu Patnaik** for their Mentorship.

I thank my parents **Y. Jaya** and **Y.V.V. Satyanarayana**.

1. Glossary of Tactics

Strategies for **TOFU (Top of the Funnel)**:

> Tactic No: 1, 5, 6, 8, 11, 13, 15, 20, 21, 25, 27, 28, 29, 31, 33, 34, 35, 36, 37, 38, 39, 40, 41, 42, 43, 44, 45, 46, 48, 50, 54, 57, 58, 59 and 61.

Strategies for **MOFU (Middle of the Funnel)**:

> Tactic No: 1, 2, 3, 6, 7, 8, 9, 10, 11, 12, 13, 15, 19, 25, 26, 27, 29, 30, 31, 32, 33, 34, 37, 38, 40, 41, 43, 45, 47, 51, 55 and 59.

Strategies for **BOFU (Bottom of the Funnel)**:

> Tactic No: 2, 3, 4, 9, 10, 11, 12, 13, 14, 15, 16, 17, 18, 19, 22, 23, 24, 25, 26, 27, 30, 32, 33, 34, 37, 40, 41, 43, 47, 49, 51, 52, 53 55, 56, 59 and 60.

Strategies using **Email**:

> Tactic No: 1, 2, 3, 5, 7, 9, 10, 13, 17, 21, 22, 25, 27, 31, 33, 37, 41, 42, 43, 45, 51, 53, 54, 56, 58 and 60.

Strategies using **Web**:

> Tactic No: 1, 2, 3, 5, 9, 10, 11, 17, 20, 21, 27, 30, 31, 33, 37, 38, 41, 42, 43, 45, 50, 53, 54, 56 and 58.

Strategies using **Direct Mail**:

> Tactic No: 1, 2, 7, 9, 12, 16, 23, 42, 43, 51, 56 and 60.

Strategies using **Event**:

> Tactic No: 2, 3, 4, 7, 8, 10, 13, 14, 16, 17, 19, 24, 27, 32, 37, 38, 41, 42,43, 45, 51, 52, 53, 54, 55, 56, 57, 58 and 60.

Strategies using **PR**:

> Tactic No: 1, 3, 10, 14, 42, 45, 52, 53, 55 and 58.

Strategies using **In-person meet**:

> Tactic No: 7, 9, 12, 16, 18, 19, 21, 22, 23, 24, 25, 37, 38, 40, 47, 49, 52, 54 and 56.

Strategies using **Tele-calling**:

> Tactic No: 2, 12, 13, 14, 21, 22, 25, 54 and 58.

Strategies using **Social Media**:

> Tactic No: 1, 2, 3, 15, 23, 29, 30, 42, 45, 50, 55, 56 and 58.

Strategies using **Martech**:

> Tactic No: 2, 8, 11, 12, 14, 15, 28, 29, 33, 34, 35, 37, 38, 39, 40, 41, 46, 49, 50, 52, 56, 57 and 61.

Strategies using **Paid Media**:

> Tactic No: 1, 3, 6, 10 and 20.

Let's Start!

2. What is ABM?

ABM Stands for Account-Based Marketing. (Account means Company). ABM is an approach where you do research, marketing, and sales activities (sometimes development and customer support also) that is very specific to selected **target accounts**.

■ *For a little more oversimplified version, here is a 2 min video:*

▶ *www.youtube.com/watch?v=OUJnsDXmOwU*

What are those specific target accounts I was referring in the previous page?

These targeted accounts are the ones that have a high probability of becoming your potential customer. This probability of being in a buying cycle is called high Propensity or high Intent.

How do you identify those specific target accounts?

Ok. Before that, we need to understand that there are two types of accounts.

1. Greenfield (net new accounts, non-customers)

2. Brownfield (existing customers)

Now coming to how to identify target accounts; Every organization has a set of parameters/criteria that denotes organizations with a high probability of becoming their customers. The fundamental need of the criteria is to act as a formula that can identify the companies that would need your product or your product category. Every organization will have a unique list of criteria based on its nature of business and target. Here are some most commonly used parameters in the criteria:

1. Industry

2. Location

3. Business Model

4. Employee Size

5. Funding amount/stage/date

6. YOY Revenue Growth

7. Technography (Tech stack)

8. IT Spend

9. Persona Growth

10. Leadership Change

11. Intent Topic Search

12. Cultural Fit

13. Procurement Approach

14. Relevance to existing clientele

15. Merger/acquisition event

16. Existing relationship with the account

17. Contract Renewal date

18. Overlap of geographic footprint

How do you target your accounts and their key stakeholders?

Through personalized communication on different channels.

What is this personalization?

ABM's no-compromise zone is customer-centric and customer-first. The intent of being personalized is to understand every account, every stakeholder in the account, understand the organization's business cases, problem statements, untapped opportunities, technological systems, objectives, roadmap, priorities, stakeholder's KRAs, KPIs, pain points, challenges... the list goes long.

The product or solution that you're going to offer has to be offered only after a thorough understanding of the account and its key stakeholder involved in the buying cycle. Ensure that you want to help them by offering relevant and connected business solutions. It's definitely not about pitching to everyone in reach.

What are the usual channels used?

The channels depend on where you find your personas (key stakeholders of the accounts) are reachable. Be it via digital medium or in-person, we look at the best time and ways to reach them. Here are some most commonly used channels:

1.   Email

2.   Tele Calling

3.   Executive Events (Roundtable)

4.   Webinar, Digital Board Room

5.   Personalized Webpage

6.   Personalized Collaterals

7.   Direct Mailer

8.   Roadshow (Account Road tour)

9.   Content Syndication

10. Industry Events Sponsorship

11. Case study/Use case on [rd] party website (gated content)

12. Social media like LinkedIn, and Twitter

13. Experiential Event

14. Online Community

15. Mobile App to access content

16. Survey Report

17. Podcast

18. One-on-one in-person meeting

19. Advisory Council Meeting

20. An executive-to-executive relationship program

21. Account-based advertising

22. Retargeting

23. Joint CSR Activity

24. Collaborative Innovation Workshop

25. In-account Day

26. Technology Day

Differences between Traditional Marketing and ABM

These differences will give you a more detailed understanding of ABM.

Traditional Marketing	Account-Based Marketing
Traditional Marketing	Account-Based Marketing
Targets a broad audience	Targets specific accounts and individuals
Mass marketing approach	Personalized and targeted approach
Focuses on lead generation	Focuses on relationship development, account acquisition and growth
One-to-many communication	One-to-one or one-to-few communication
Limited or no personalization	Highly personalized messaging and content
Emphasizes quantity of leads	Emphasizes quality of accounts
Broad reach across various industries	Narrow focus on high-value target accounts
ROI measured based on lead generation	ROI measured based on account revenue
Marketing and sales operate separately	Marketing, sales and other revenue teams collaborate closely

Here is how the concept of ABM has come to the marketing world (Flashback):

ABM is the evolution of the concept, customer-centric marketing.

Year 2002 **Year 2003** **Year 2009**

A book named "The One to One Future" was released. This talks about building relationships with customers & this book revolutionized theB2B marketing.

By this year, some top global Companies have pioneered Client centric marketing approach.

The word "Account Based Marketing" is coined by ITSMA.

ABM was fine tuned with more collaborative planning that made the approach more cross-functional.

Year 2011 **Year 2012** **Year 2016**

Automation has set its foot into ABM, starting with the activity of doing research and gathering information of companies and prospects.

Four stages of ABM Adoption has been introduced. Made ABM more adoptable with the frictionless process of exploration, piloting, scaling up and embedding ABM program into organizations.

The concept of "3 types of ABM" has been introduced.

3. Types of ABM

The three types of ABM have different approaches and different resource intensities. Here comes the three types of ABM approaches:

1. **<u>One-to-one ABM (Strategic ABM):</u>** In a one-to-one ABM program only a few high-value accounts are selected to target with personalized marketing campaigns. This approach is highly focused and requires a deep understanding of the targeted accounts to create customized marketing strategies that resonate with the decision-makers in those accounts. One-to-one ABM is typically used for accounts that generate a significant portion of a company's revenue.

2. **<u>One-to-few ABM (Lite ABM):</u>** In a one-to-few ABM program, a small group of accounts with similar characteristics and needs are targeted. The marketing strategies used for each account are tailored to their specific requirements while also taking into account the commonalities between them. One-to-few ABM is more scalable than one-to-one ABM, as companies can target multiple accounts with similar marketing tactics.

3. **<u>One-to-many ABM (Programmatic ABM):</u>** In a one-to-many ABM program, larger group of accounts that share common characteristics, such as being in the same industry or having similar business needs are targeted. The marketing strategies used for each account are more generalized and less personalized than in one-to-one or one-to-few ABM. This approach is best for companies that are looking to expand their customer base and want to target a wider range of potential accounts.

Now, to earn even better clarity, let's find out the differences between these three ABM types.

ABM Type	One-to-One	One-to-Few	One-to-Many
Number of Accounts per SDR	10-20	40-50	500-1000 (no SDR allocated)
Content Personalization	50-80% new content & messaging for this account personas	25-50% Customizing existing content and messaging for every account	10-15% Content & messaging specific at Industry or segment level
Research	At account level	At cluster level	At industry level
Audience	All account key stakeholders	All account key stakeholders	ICP
In-person interactions	✓	✓	✓
Direct Mailer	✓	✓	✗
Webinar	✗	✗	✓
Web Personalization	✓	✓	✓
Retargeting	✓	✓	✓
Pre-targeted advertising	✓	✓	✗
Executive Event	✓	✓	✗
Email	✓	✓	✓
Tele calling	✓	✓	✗
Advisory Council	✓	✗	✗
Thought Leadership Promotions	✓	✓	✗
Content Syndication	✓	✓	✓

ABM Type	One-to-One	One-to-Few	One-to-Many
Targeting stages	TOFU, MOFU, BOFU	TOFU, MOFU, BOFU	TOFU, MOFU,
Account Scoring	✓	✓	✓
Metrics	Tactical & Business Outcome	Tactical & Business Outcome	Tactical
Personalized Advert	✓	✓	✗
Dedicated Resources	✓	✓	✗
Brownfield Accounts	✓	✓	✗
Greenfield Accounts	✓	✓	✓
Perception Interviews	✓	✓	✗
Innovation Workshops	✓	✗	✗
Session with SME	✓	✓	✗
Customized Offerings	✓	✗	✗

What is NOT ABM?

To avoid misconceptions or wrong expectations, it is equally important for us to know what is not ABM or what should not be expected under your ABM programs.

1. ABM is not just a marketing initiative, it is a companywide change initiative with the involvement of teams such as Sales, Marketing, Customer Success, Customer Support, Product Development and Leadership.

2. ABM program is not a one-man army or one-department army to go ahead and start. Unlike Demand Generation or any other traditional marketing approaches, ABM involves in every stage of the funnel (or flywheel).

3. ABM is not a typical funnel-filling tactic like Demand generation or lead generation. ABM aims at building relationships which is a long-term approach.

4. Unless you understand the core intention and approach of ABM, you cannot measure the performance of your ABM. It is easy to mistake ABM for measuring like you do Demand Gen. Based on the stage of the ABM program, the type of ABM, its objective and the resources involved, the performance of the program can be measured with various metrics.

5. ABM is not a quantitative approach but a qualitative approach. It doesn't focus on the number of leads generated but on the quality of leads.

6. ABM is not just for net new account but also for existing accounts. Increasing the Customer Lifetime Value and exploring account growth opportunities are one of the most important objectives of ABM programs.

7. Every ABM program (except programmatic type) has both greenfield and brownfield accounts with a ratio of 40:60 to 60:40. Needless to say that it is always smart to leverage the accounts with growth opportunities.

8. ABM is neither product-centric nor organization-centric, it is customer-centric. It doesn't work out on the inside-out approach but on the outside-in culture.

9. Without the culture of customer-centric in an organization running an ABM program would make the ABM program eventually a demand generation program by losing its purpose and edge of understanding and playing along with the market demands.

4. Stages of ABM

Understanding the stages of ABM in its life cycle will give you not only a helicopter view of the ABM process but also gives you the ability to focus on the specific stage when you want to monitor, measure or even repair your ABM program.

1. Foundation of the ABM Program

2. Identifying Accounts and Key stakeholders

3. Connect and engage with key stakeholders of target accounts

4. Measure the ABM program at an account and program level.

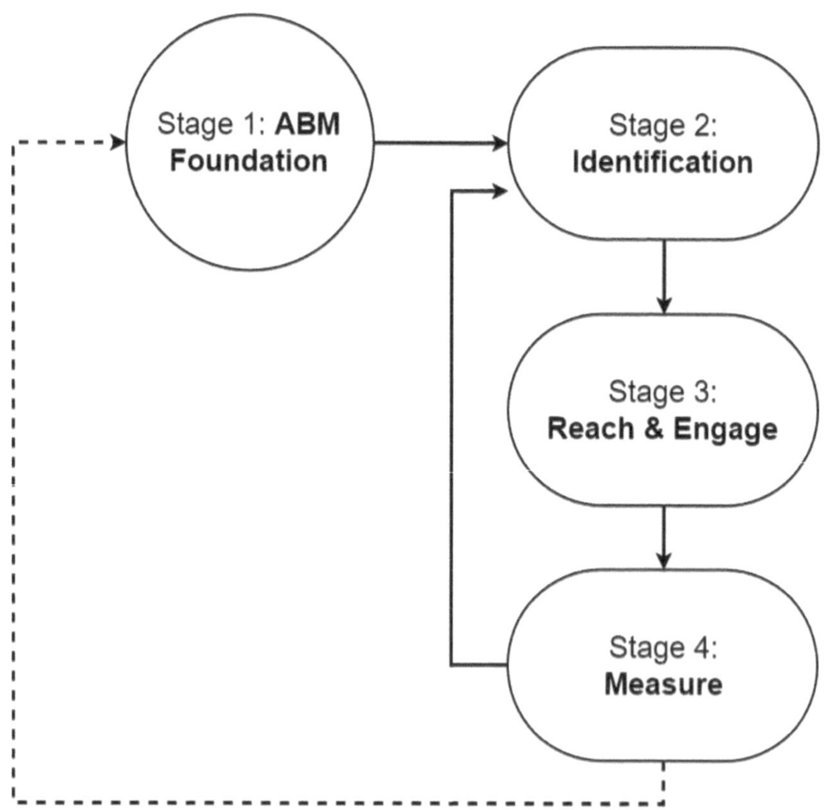

Stage 1: ABM Foundation

The Objective of this stage is to establish the foundation of Account-Based Marketing (ABM) programs. Gaining a comprehensive and accurate view of your prospects and customers plays a crucial role in unifying data and delivering appropriate experiences to the target accounts. The foundation work also involves establishing criteria and scoring methodologies to evaluate the propensity or intent of an account towards your product or product category.

Creating a foundation for your ABM program involves

a.   Defining Account scoring parameters and methods.

b.   Integrating and unifying data from multiple teams, channels and activities.

c.   Data access and governance

a. Define Scoring: Does it sound very obvious if I say to achieve our goal, we need to identify the target? It might sound so, but here with ABM, identifying targets plays a very important role. Because choosing the wrong accounts could drain all your resources, time and efforts and can leave your entire ABM program at risk.

To avoid this risk, we define our criteria that identify the high propensity accounts (potential accounts that have a high probability of buying our product).

These criteria can include various factors such as firmographics (company size, industry, location), technographics (technology stack, infrastructure), intent data (online behaviour, search activity), and other relevant indicators. The goal is to identify the characteristics and signals that indicate an account's potential interest in your offerings.

Once the scoring criteria and data sources are established, a scoring methodology needs to be developed.

The scoring method involves assigning weights and values to each criterion based on its relevance and significance. By applying the scoring methodology to the account data, you can generate a numeric score or propensity index that indicates the account's inclination towards your product or product category.

b. Data Integration: Once the criteria to identify your target accounts have been established, we will focus on building a data strategy that accommodates all our ABM program activities.

The objective is to unify data that is coming from various sources like channels, teams and tools and also build a comprehensive view that can make the data more actionable. This includes leveraging both internal data (CRM, CDP, marketing automation, sales data) and external data (third-party data providers, intent data platforms) to gather a wide range of information about the accounts. Data integration ensures that you have a complete and accurate understanding of each account's attributes and behaviours.

c. Data Access and Governance: Now that we have built our criteria to identify our target accounts, and a framework to capture data and make it comprehensive, now we shall aim at making this data more accessible.

The very purpose of data is to be insightful and actionable, isn't it? This important aspect of the account data foundation ensures that every stakeholder involved has access to a single view of the account data to the right degree of need.

Data foundation demands implementing data governance practices to maintain data quality, consistency, and accessibility. Data governance includes processes for data cleansing, standardization, deduplication, and ongoing data management to prevent data discrepancies and ensure data integrity.

As the sources of data, the channels of communication, personalization tactics and measuring metrics keep evolving, the data strategy has to evolve to keep up with them.

The Bottom line: Though the ABM foundation sounds like a one-time activity it needs continuous refinement and adaptation as new data becomes available and market dynamics change. Regularly reviewing and updating the scoring criteria, data sources, and scoring methodologies based on feedback, insights, and performance analysis is crucial to maintain the effectiveness of your ABM program.

By establishing an account data foundation, you can have a unified and comprehensive view of your prospects and customers, enabling you to prioritize and target the right accounts effectively. It serves as the basis for personalized and targeted ABM strategies, ensuring that your marketing and sales efforts are aligned with the much-needed specific needs and interests of each account.

Stage 2: Identify Accounts & Key Stakeholders

The Objective of this stage is to identify the best accounts with a high probability of needing your product or product category or any other alternate solution to the problem that your product addresses.

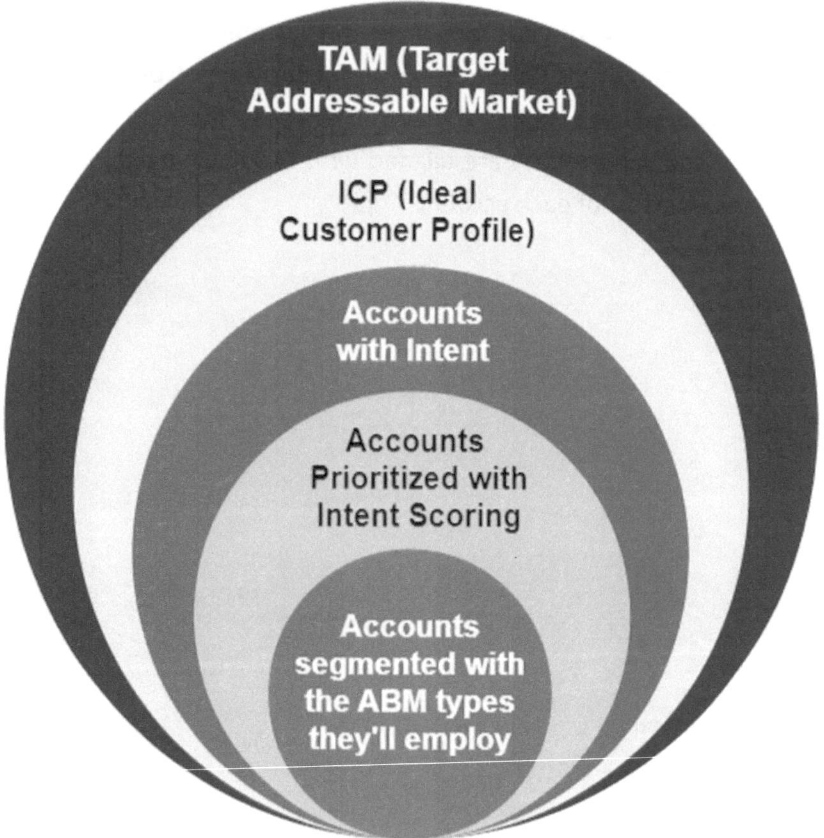

The image in the previous images depicts the scope of your target market at various focal lengths.

1.   **Total Addressable Market (TAM) Analysis:** Total Addressable Market refers to the total number of potential customers or accounts that fit within your target market. This involves analysing industry data, market research, and internal data to estimate the size and scope of

your potential customer base. A simple way of finding out the TAM is using Linkedin campaign manager or Linkedin search or even Google Ads campaign tool.

2. **Ideal Customer Profile (ICP):** Once you have a clear understanding of your TAM, the next step is to define your Ideal Customer Profile. This involves identifying the specific characteristics, attributes, and firmographics of the accounts that are most likely to derive value from your product or solution. This includes factors such as company size, industry, revenue, geographic location, technology stack, and other relevant criteria.

    ICP is nothing but the TAM that is more pragmatically in reach with respect to your product and organization's positioning in the market.

3. **Accounts with Intent**: But, do we have the bandwidth to reach and put efforts on every account that fits in our ICP? No! This is when we have to distill our focus further.

    Intent is the way to distill our focus further. We use intent to identify accounts that show signals of interest in your product or solution. This can be done by monitoring various sources of intent data, such as website visits, content downloads, social media activity, search behaviour, 3rd party content syndication, 3rd party intent data and engagement with your marketing campaigns.

    By tracking these intent signals, you can identify accounts that are actively researching or showing interest in your product category. Establishing various resources can make your target account list more reliable.

4. **Intent Scoring**: Once you have identified accounts with intent, we've to score them. We can say, this is further distillation with the purpose of choosing in which accounts you would want to put your resources wisely.

    The intent scoring assigns a numeric score to each account based on the intensity and frequency of their intent signals. The scoring can be done using various intent data platforms, machine learning algorithms, or a combination of manual assessment and data analysis. Intent scoring helps prioritize accounts based on their level of engagement and interest.

One min video on scoring*: youtube.com/shorts/kSR7PKVFEDk*

5. **Account Segmentation**: Based on the intent scores and their estimated opportunities, we need to segment the accounts into different categories or tiers. This segmentation can be based on criteria such as intent level, industry segments, revenue ranges, growth potential, purchase history, market share, and the value they can bring to your business. Account segmentation is all bucketing the accounts into various ABM programs with different approaches such as one-to-one, one-to-few and one-to-many.

Stage 3: Connect and Engage

The Objective of this stage is to understand the key stakeholders of your target accounts, right to their pain points, priorities, KRAs, KPIs, challenges, etc. and make more meaningful conversations with them. This involves reaching them with high personalization communications based on the ABM program the account is enrolled into. This targeted approach increases the chances of successful engagement by driving meaningful conversations with the right individuals within your target accounts.

1. **Identify Key Stakeholders:** The key stakeholders are the individuals who have the power to influence or make decisions at any stage of the buying process. They could be executives, managers, department heads, or other relevant roles depending on the organization and industry. Conducting thorough research and leveraging your existing contacts can help identify the right stakeholders for each account.

2. **Research and Understanding:** Once the key stakeholders are identified, in-depth research on each stakeholder is performed.

This includes understanding their roles, responsibilities, pain points, priorities, key performance indicators (KPIs), challenges and goals. Research can be done through various channels such as their LinkedIn profiles, company websites, industry publications, press releases, resumes and other publicly available information.

3. **Account-Based Messaging and Personalization:** With the research insights in hand, the next step is to craft account-based messaging that helps in personalizing the communication for each stakeholder. This involves tailoring your value proposition, messaging, and content to align with the specific pain points, priorities, and objectives of each stakeholder.

    It is crucial to create compelling and relevant messages that resonate with their organization and individual, needs, opportunities and challenges. Personalization does not just include addressing the stakeholder by name, referencing their specific role or responsibilities, but also highlighting how your solution can address their unique requirements or expectations.

4. **ABM Type and Channel Selection:** Based on the ABM type you are using for a particular account (one-to-one, one-to-few, or one-to-many), you need to determine the most effective channels to reach the identified stakeholders. The channels include emails, targeted social media campaigns, direct mail, phone calls, in-person meeting, events and others. The goal of this step is to select the channels that will have the highest impact and engagement with the stakeholders.

5. **Engage and Nurture:** Once the personalized messaging and communication channels are determined, it's time to outreach, engage the stakeholders and nurture the relationship. This involves initiating conversations that address their pain points, showcase your expertise, and provide relevant content or resources that can add value to their specific challenges. Regular follow-ups and ongoing communication are key to building trust and maintaining the relationship.

Stage 4: Measure (Metrics of ABM Program)

The Objective of this stage is to measure the success of an Account-Based Marketing (ABM) program. Measurement can be done at both the account level and program level by assessing various key performance indicators (KPIs) and tracking the progress of accounts.

Account-Level Measurement:

1. **Number of Contacts:** Track the number of key stakeholders within target accounts that have been profiled and reached.

2. **Engagement Rate:** Measure the level of engagement from key stakeholders, such as email open rates, click-through rates, event attendance, and content downloads. This helps gauge the effectiveness of your personalized communication.

3. **Accounts Visited Website:** Monitor the number of prospects from target accounts who have visited your website, indicating their interest and engagement.

4. **Event Attendance:** Measure the participation of a target account through their registration and attendance of an in-person or online event.

5. **Ad Clicks:** Monitor the number of clicks on targeted advertisements by individuals from the target accounts.

6. **Social Media Engagement:** Track social media interactions, such as likes, comments, and shares, from key stakeholders within the target accounts.

Other metrics are propensity, no of decision makers connected by Sales, pipe value, pipe velocity, account coverage, win rate, no of meetings and stage of the account (w.r.t the customer journey map).

Program-Level Measurement:

1. **Number of Accounts at various stages**: Measure the number of target accounts that are at various stages, right from becoming the target account to converting it into a customer and upselling or cross-selling.

2. **Pipeline Value:** Assess the total pipe value of the deals associated with the target accounts in the pipe.

3. **Account Progression Speed Aka Pipe Velocity:** Track the speed of the progress of accounts at different stages of the sales cycle, such as initial contact, qualification, proposal, negotiation, and closed-won.

4. **Revenue Generated:** Measure the revenue generated from the ABM program's target accounts.

5. **Customer Lifetime Value (CLV):** Analyze the long-term value of customers and their potential for upselling and cross-selling.

6. **Customer Satisfaction and Retention:** Monitor customer satisfaction and retention rates among the accounts targeted through ABM efforts.

Remember that what you don't measure cannot be improved. It is essential to use a combination of quantitative and qualitative measures to evaluate the success of your ABM program. This includes tracking specific metrics and KPIs, analysing data from different channels and touchpoints, and gathering feedback from both the sales team and key stakeholders.

Regular reporting and analysis of these metrics will help you understand the impact of your ABM program, identify areas for improvement, and make data-driven decisions to optimize your efforts.

60+ ABM Tactics

Tactic #1: Repack Your Solution Flyers into Industry Playbook

Stage of Funnel: TOFU   MOFU

Channels Involved: Email, Web, Direct Mailer, Event and 3rd party Web (Content Syndication)

Tactic Description: One effective way to engage potential B2B clients is to reframe your product or service collateral as a valuable resource for their industry. Rather than simply promoting your own offerings, you can create a playbook or book of business cases, trends, and insights that highlight key challenges, trends, and solutions for your target audience.

Example: Microsoft's "Book of Dreams" offers industry-specific editions tailored to manufacturing, healthcare, airlines, banking, and other sectors. By offering practical insights and thought leadership on industry-specific topics, Microsoft positioned itself as a partner rather than just a vendor. (*Source: https://www.6sc.com/book-of-dreams/*)

Insights:

1. Collate the existing content and repackage it appropriately to the industry. If your existing content is not sufficient, add new valuable content.

2. The created sub-brand can be used for other activities like video series, webpages, events, etc.

3. You can repeat this yearly or once in two years based on the new content of insights you've got to publish.

Execution Steps:

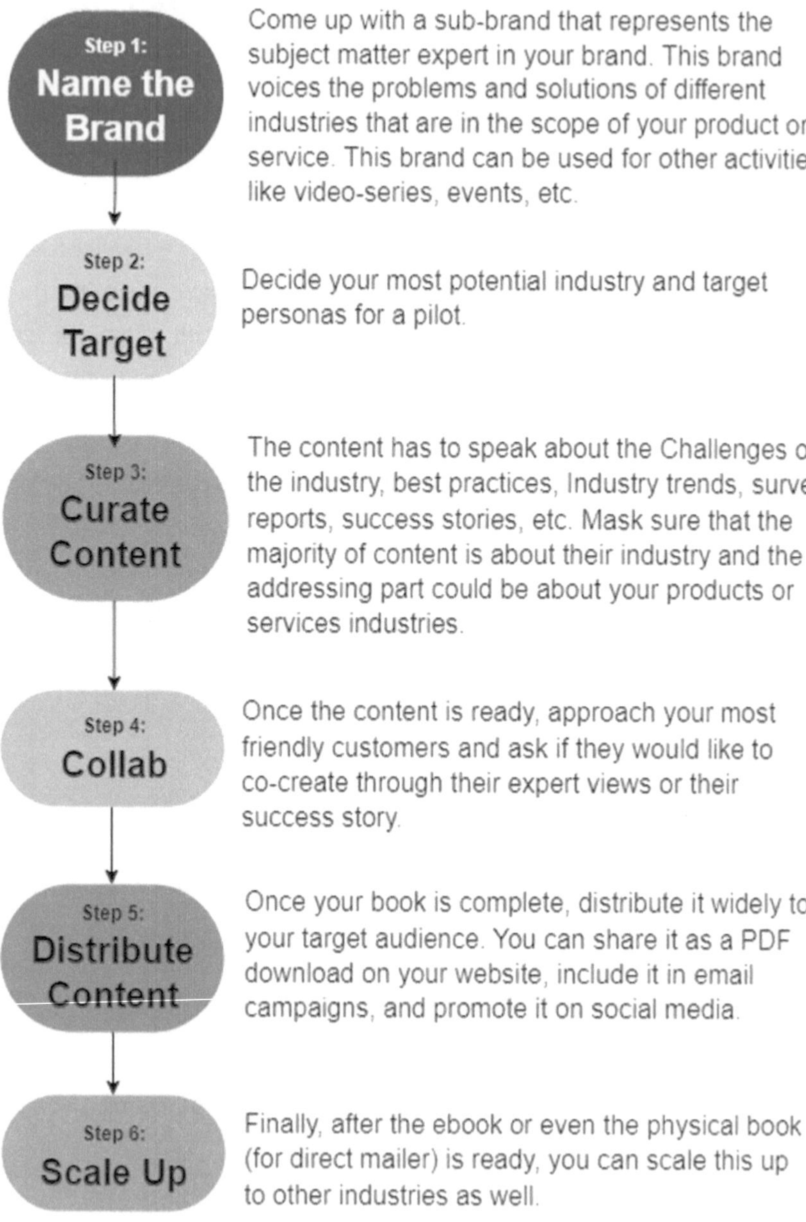

Come up with a sub-brand that represents the subject matter expert in your brand. This brand voices the problems and solutions of different industries that are in the scope of your product or service. This brand can be used for other activities like video-series, events, etc.

Decide your most potential industry and target personas for a pilot.

The content has to speak about the Challenges of the industry, best practices, Industry trends, survey reports, success stories, etc. Mask sure that the majority of content is about their industry and the addressing part could be about your products or services industries.

Once the content is ready, approach your most friendly customers and ask if they would like to co-create through their expert views or their success story.

Once your book is complete, distribute it widely to your target audience. You can share it as a PDF download on your website, include it in email campaigns, and promote it on social media.

Finally, after the ebook or even the physical book (for direct mailer) is ready, you can scale this up to other industries as well.

Tactic #2: Experiential events for executives from key accounts

Stage of Funnel: TOFU   MOFU

Channels Involved: Event

Tactic Description: In today's fast-paced age, executives are constantly bombarded with an overwhelming number of events such as webinars, roundtables, and conferences. It's harder and harder to get their presence at the same old format events, and if it's your high-priority account, you need to stand out and make a lasting impression.

Experiential events offer a unique opportunity to create a memorable and personal experience for your prospects. These events go beyond the traditional business-focused roundtable discussions and instead offer a chance to build relationships and connections in a more relaxed and enjoyable environment. This would be the right time for them to open up and share their pain points and expectations.

Some of the experiential activities included:

1.   Golf Experience

2.   Hot air balloon ride

3.   Hosting a cooking class with a celebrity as the chief guest

4.   Racing events

5.   Sports events like the IPL, Super Bowl, and World Cups

6.   Jungle Stay

7.   Cruise Journey

8.   Wellness retreats

9.   Interactive Workshops

<u>Example:</u> A SAAS company hosted a 3-day wellness retreat for their top 10 prospects and their families. Set against a serene seaside resort, the retreat offered relaxation, spa treatments, and family-friendly activities. This event was a mix of personal activities, such as spa, local sightseeing, and business activities such as workshop & round table. The event fostered strong relationships and left a lasting impression.

Execution Steps:

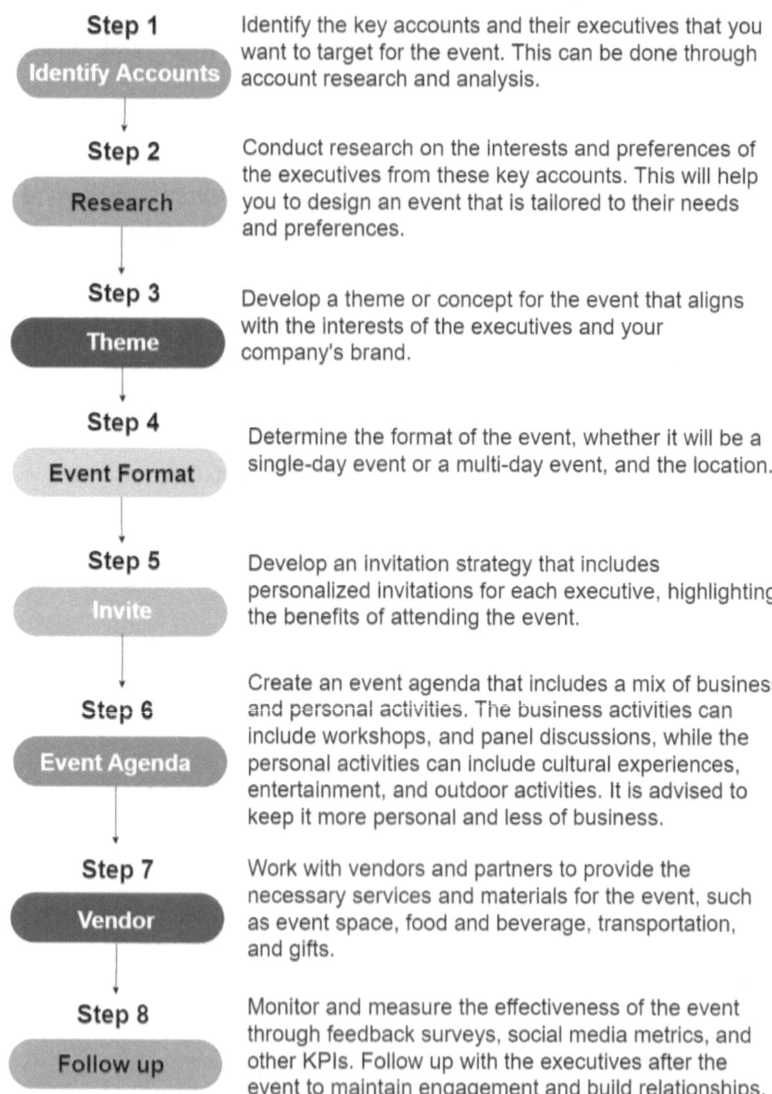

Step 1 — Identify Accounts: Identify the key accounts and their executives that you want to target for the event. This can be done through account research and analysis.

Step 2 — Research: Conduct research on the interests and preferences of the executives from these key accounts. This will help you to design an event that is tailored to their needs and preferences.

Step 3 — Theme: Develop a theme or concept for the event that aligns with the interests of the executives and your company's brand.

Step 4 — Event Format: Determine the format of the event, whether it will be a single-day event or a multi-day event, and the location.

Step 5 — Invite: Develop an invitation strategy that includes personalized invitations for each executive, highlighting the benefits of attending the event.

Step 6 — Event Agenda: Create an event agenda that includes a mix of business and personal activities. The business activities can include workshops, and panel discussions, while the personal activities can include cultural experiences, entertainment, and outdoor activities. It is advised to keep it more personal and less of business.

Step 7 — Vendor: Work with vendors and partners to provide the necessary services and materials for the event, such as event space, food and beverage, transportation, and gifts.

Step 8 — Follow up: Monitor and measure the effectiveness of the event through feedback surveys, social media metrics, and other KPIs. Follow up with the executives after the event to maintain engagement and build relationships.

Tactic #3: Thought Leadership Promotion through Success Story

Stage of Funnel: MOFU   BOFU

Channels Involved: Email, Web, Paid Media, Social Media, Event and PR.

Tactic Description: One effective way to establish thought leadership and build credibility with potential customers is by sharing the success stories of existing customers. This tactic involves showcasing how your product or service has helped a customer achieve their goals, which in turn can inspire and attract new prospects.

Channels:

- Social media

- Email

- Video

- Webpage: Media Publications

- Blog

- Community Channels

- Award Ceremony

- In-account Day event

Content Formats:

- Long content format (Webpage, Blog Post)

- Testimonial

- Customer Success Story and Case Study

- Business Cases, Industry Insight

- Video Interview

- Podcasts

Example: A leading technology company invited its top five customers to an exclusive industry event, providing them with an opportunity for a joint interview alongside subject matter experts from both the customer and the technology company. The insightful video interview was strategically promoted across multiple channels, highlighting the thought leadership of both the customer and the technology company.

Execution Steps:

5 steps to Thought Leadership Promotion

1. Identify key success stories

Identify your customers who have achieved significant success using your product or service and reach put to them.

2. Create compelling content

Develop compelling content in various formats around these success stories, such as case studies, testimonials, or videos.

3. Distribute the content strategically

Identify the channels to distribute it strategically. This could involve sharing the content via email, social media, or even hosting a webinar or an in-person meet or a virtual event to showcase the customer success story.

4. Leverage personalization

Use the success story to tailor your messaging to your target accounts and show how your solution can help them achieve similar success.

5. Track metrics

Finally, track the metrics to measure the impact of your success story campaign. This could include the number of views, engagement rates, or even the number of qualified leads generated as a result of the campaign.

Tactic #4: Collaborative Ideation Workshop: Unleashing Innovation with Key Accounts

Stage of Funnel: BOFU

Channels Involved: Event

Tactic Description: The ABM tactic of doing an ideation or brainstorming workshop with customers or key targeted accounts can be a great way to build strong relationships and generate new ideas that can help drive business growth.

Workshop Formats:

1. A design thinking workshop is a structured approach to problem-solving that encourages creativity and collaboration.

2. A meet post-technical system research and processes research on the account.

3. Can be combined with recreational activities.

4. Can be made into a breakout session of your customer success summit.

5. Can include a third party such as McKinsey or IDC which makes it more attractive and valuable.

6. Can be clubbed into an award function as well.

Ways of delivering Value:

1. Pictures with the frame to all the participants

2. Well-framed videos of the workshop that highlight signification quotes

3. Storifying their so-far journey and visualising the near future. This story has to depict everything from their road map to the next action item.

Example: A digital transformation solution company has hosted an innovation workshop with a conglomerate. After detailed research on the target account, this workshop has exclusively focused on addressing their concerns, untapped opportunities and a roadmap that is in alignment with their business cases and overall business strategy.

Execution Steps:

1. Identify Key Accounts

Start by identifying your key accounts and selecting the ones that would be the most interested in participating in a brainstorming workshop.

2. Set up the Workshop

Once you have your list of customers, set up a workshop with them where you can brainstorm and ideate together. This can be done either in-person or virtually, depending on what works best for everyone.

3. Record the workshop

As you conduct the workshop, be sure to record the session so that you can capture all of the valuable insights and ideas that are generated. You can either record the session on video or take notes, but video is preferred as it is more engaging.

4. Design the Content

Once the workshop is finished, pick up the insights brainstormed and the action items discussed. Using these, make a presentation in the form of video bytes, infographics, detailed roadmap suggested action items, etc. You can also add some branding to the presentation.

5. Share the Content

Once the video or ebook or a report or content in any other format is edited, share it with your account team and the customers who participated in the workshop. This will not only help you build stronger relationships with your customers, but it will also help you position your company as a thought leader in our industry.

Tactic #5: Personalized Video Email

Stage of Funnel: TOFU

Channels Involved: Email and Web

Tactic Description: The idea behind this tactic is to create a customized video message that addresses the key accounts by their name and company name and deliver it to them via email.

The video thumbnail should also be personalized to communicate that the video was made specifically for them. This can help you stand out from the crowd of generic emails that your key accounts receive daily.

The key to making this tactic successful is to create a video that is tailored to the specific interests and pain points of each key account. This requires thorough research and a deep understanding of your key accounts' businesses and industries. Or at least you can cluster your accounts based on industry, their common challenges or any key common trait that unites them.

In the video, you can share insights or solutions that are relevant to the key account's cluster-specific needs, and show how your company can help them achieve their goals. This can help build a stronger connection with your key accounts and demonstrate our commitment to their success.

Example (an Email):

Hi Sai Krishna, I recorded this 1-minute video for you with an idea on how to get more clients like <existing client name> for your organization.

Open to hearing more?

Cheers,

<sender>

Execution Steps:

Step 1

Depending upon your ability to address organizations at an individual level or at a cluster level or at an industry level, decide the segmentation of accounts. Make sure that the accounts are a good fit for your product or service and that they have a genuine need for it.

Step 2

Create a personalized video message that is tailored to each segment. The message should be short, concise, and engaging, and it should highlight the key benefits of your product or service.

Step 3

Create a personalized video message that is tailored to each segment. The message should be short, concise, and engaging, and it should highlight the key benefits of your product or service.

Step 4

Craft a personalized email for each key account that includes a link to the video. The subject line should be attention-grabbing and should clearly communicate the value of the video.

Step 5

Using tool like NeuralSynAI through which you can automate the video production for all the organizations and people you're addressing in the video. The thumbnail should be visually appealing and should clearly communicate that the video is personalized for the key account.

Tactic #6: The Dynamic Duo: Pre-targeting and Retargeting

Stage of Funnel: TOFU   MOFU

Channels Involved: Paid Media and 3rd party Web.

Tactic Description: Pre-targeting and retargeting are two powerful tactics that can be used in an ABM program to reach and engage with key accounts. Pre-targeting involves targeting potential customers with specific ads or content before they visit your website or take any action. This can help to build awareness and interest in your brand, as well as create a more targeted audience for your retargeting efforts.

Retargeting involves targeting people who have already engaged with your brand or website and encouraging them to take further action. This can include nurturing them with additional content, promoting offers or discounts, or inviting them to participate in events or webinars.

When used together, pre-targeting and retargeting can create a comprehensive ABM strategy that spans the entire customer journey, from awareness to advocacy.

Use pre-targeting for both awareness and driving action stages and retargeting for both nurturing and advocacy stages.

Ways to Pre-targeting and Retargeting:

1.   Account-based advertising on Linkedin or using tools such as Recotap, Rollworks and other Programmatic Advertising.

2.   Use tools such as Google Optimize or VWO for personalizing the web experience after clicking the ad.

Execution Steps:

Step 1: Identify potential accounts: Start by identifying potential accounts that have a higher intent to purchase your product or service. Look for accounts that have shown interest in your brand, visited your website, or engaged with your content. Use an ideal customer profile (ICP) genome to identify accounts that match your ideal customer characteristics. Additionally, use retargeting to reach out to accounts that have already shown interest in your brand.

Step 2: Segment accounts: Once you have identified potential accounts, segment them into clusters based on their content inclinations. This step will involve analyzing the content that they have engaged with in the past and grouping them into clusters of accounts that have a common interest in certain types of content.

Step 3: Personalize data: Now that you have segmented accounts into clusters, it's time to personalize the data for each cluster. Use the data that you have collected to personalize your messaging and content to align with each cluster's interests and preferences. This could include personalized emails, videos, or ads that are tailored to each cluster.

Step 4: Engage targeted accounts: Use a combination of retargeting and pre-targeting to engage the targeted accounts with your personalized content. Retargeting involves showing ads or content to accounts that have already engaged with your brand, while pretargeting involves showing ads to accounts that fit your ideal customer profile but haven't engaged with your brand yet. This comprehensive approach will help to ensure that your targeted accounts are engaged at every stage of the customer journey.

Pretarget Objectives

a) Build Awareness
b) Engage with your target accounts

→

Retarget Objectives

a) Nurture accounts in pipe
b) Build customer advocates

Tactic #7: Personalized Collaterals

Stage of Funnel: MOFU

Channels Involved: Event, In-person meet, Email and Direct Mailer.

Tactic Description: When a meeting is scheduled with your target account, you can design personalized brochures and presentations that match their colour palette and imagery. This will create a more cohesive and memorable experience for the prospect.

Example: A Fintech company specializing in financial solutions targeted a few high-value accounts in the banking sector. They invited the key decision-makers of these accounts to an executive event. With thorough research on the accounts before the event, they were able to create a personalized and impactful experience for the prospects during the event.

They designed personalized collaterals while incorporating the account's colour palette, fonts, and imagery into the design to ensure a consistent and visually appealing experience that aligned with the prospect's brand.

In addition to visual customization, the Fintech company tailored the content of the brochures and presentations to address the specific needs and challenges faced by the account. They highlighted relevant case studies and success stories to showcase their expertise and demonstrate how their solutions could help the bank achieve its objectives.

They paid attention to details such as paper quality, finishes, and packaging. The collateral was professionally assembled and presented in branded folders or sleek packaging to create a polished and professional impression. To ensure hyper-personalization they have collected some collaterals of the accounts and use them as a reference to ensure their design reflects the target account's aesthetics.

Execution Steps:

Step 1: Research the account

Once your account with meeting has been identified, do a research on their language on website, social media, brand imagery and color palette.

Step 2: Hyper Personalize

Personalize brochures and presentations that match their color palette, language and imagery. This will create a more cohesive and memorable experience for the prospect.

Step 3: Add Value

It's important to incorporate personalization into the content, not just the design. This means tailoring the messaging, examples, and case studies or business cases to match the prospect's specific needs and pain points.

Step 4: Channels

Deliver personalized content through various channels such as email, direct mail, pre-targeted ads, events, or in-person meetings.

Tactic #8: Crack the tough nuts through Industry Events

Stage of Funnel: TOFU   MOFU

Channels Involved: Event

Tactic Description: This tactic helps when you're having trouble reaching certain key accounts and getting their meeting or any opportunity to present. This is about sponsoring an industry summit, getting your non-reachable prospects invited as delegates or panelists and having a one-on-one meeting.

Example: A B2B software company had been struggling to secure meetings and engage with key accounts in the healthcare industry. They decided to leverage industry events to connect with their non-responsive prospects.

They have segmented their cold, hostile and significant accounts based on their industry or the types of events the key stakeholders would be interested in. Then they identified the right industry summits focused on the interests of the target accounts.

They have sponsored the events with a wish list of accounts to be invited to the events. Not only have they gotten their chance to interact with their accounts, but also showcased their expertise, increased brand awareness, and positioned themselves as industry leaders.

As part of the sponsorship package, the organizers delivered One-on-one meetings, keynote sessions, panel discussions and breakout sessions such as roundtables and conferences.

By sponsoring events and securing invitations for their non-responsive prospects, the company successfully broke through communication barriers. They leveraged the event as a platform to establish thought leadership, made meaningful connections, showcased their expertise, and gained valuable face-to-face interactions.

Execution Steps:

Step 1

Maintain a Segment of potential accounts that have turn cold or hostile.

Step 2

Sponsor an industry summit with deliverables of your priority audiences (your cold but important audience list) break-out sessions, one-on-one meetings, thought leadership video bytes, booth space, and others.

Step 3

As you see the registrations, keep your personalized collaterals ready along with research ground work for your interactions.

Step 4

Give them a white glove experience through personalized gifting. This serves as a nice ice breaking session.

Tactic #9: Account-Based Business Case Development

Stage of Funnel: MOFU BOFU

Channels Involved: Email, Web, In-person meet and Event.

Tactic Description: This tactic involves creating a detailed business case that speaks to the unique needs and challenges of the target organization, rather than providing a one-size-fits-all solution. We're bound to provide value to customers even before they become our customers. Many times, value can be added by giving them business cases that will help them.

Example: A management consulting firm conducted in-depth research and analysis to understand the unique needs and challenges of their top priority target account. They tailored the business cases to address specific pain points and provide actionable insights for their organization. These valuable insights, roadmaps and calls to action were documented through the personalized collateral. This demonstrated their commitment to delivering value.

Based on the insights gathered, the consultancy developed personalized business use cases for each target organization. These business use cases highlighted how their management consulting services could address the prospect's unique challenges and help them achieve their strategic goals. They showcased previous success stories, industry benchmarks, and relevant case studies to support their recommendations.

In addition to the business use cases, the consultancy shared valuable insights, recommendations, best practices and market insights to further illustrate their understanding of the client's context and the potential impact of their consulting services.

Execution Steps:

Step 1: Research the target Organization

Conduct in-depth research on the target organization, including its industry, competitors, products, and recent news or announcements. The sources of research could be their annual/quarterly reports, your own CRM, Intent data, their website, press coverage, social media posts, blog articles, events, Industry analyst reports, Contract renewal database, information from account managers.

Step 2: Identify Key Stakeholder

Determine the key decision-makers and influencers within the target organization, and understand their priorities and pain points. Develop detailed buyer profiles for every stakeholder that talks about their professional journey, personal inclinations, their KPIs, KRAs, etc.

Step 3: Tailor the business case

Develop a customized business case that addresses the specific needs and challenges of the target organization. This may include showcasing how your product or service can solve a particular problem or help achieve specific goals.

Step 4: Provide proof points

Use data, case studies, and customer testimonials to support your claims and provide proof points that your solution is effective and can deliver results.

Step 5: Personalize the delivery

Deliver the business case in a way that resonates with the target organization, such as through a personalized presentation, one-on-one meeting, or tailored content.

Tactic #10: Pipe Acceleration Activities

Stage of Funnel: MOFU   BOFU

Channels Involved: Email, Web, Paid Media, Social Media and Event.

Tactic Description: This tactic involves activities to progress the leads in the pipe that have been stuck or that need a push to go towards becoming customers. Pipeline acceleration also refers to the process of speeding up the sales cycle and shortening the time it takes for a lead to become a customer.

You can make multiple lists of prospects based on their propensity and potential and therefore map them to multiple marketing activities. Your pipe acceleration activities will be part of your account plan.

Once you identify the list of accounts that have to be accelerated, here is what to do...

Example: A leading IT consultancy identified leads in their pipeline that were experiencing delays or showing signs of being stuck in the sales process. They further categorized the leads into different lists based on their likelihood of conversion and their potential impact on revenue growth.

The pipe acceleration activities were integrated into the overall micro-cluster plan for each segment. The plans outlined the strategies, tactics, and resources dedicated to nurturing and converting the leads into clients.

Execution Steps:

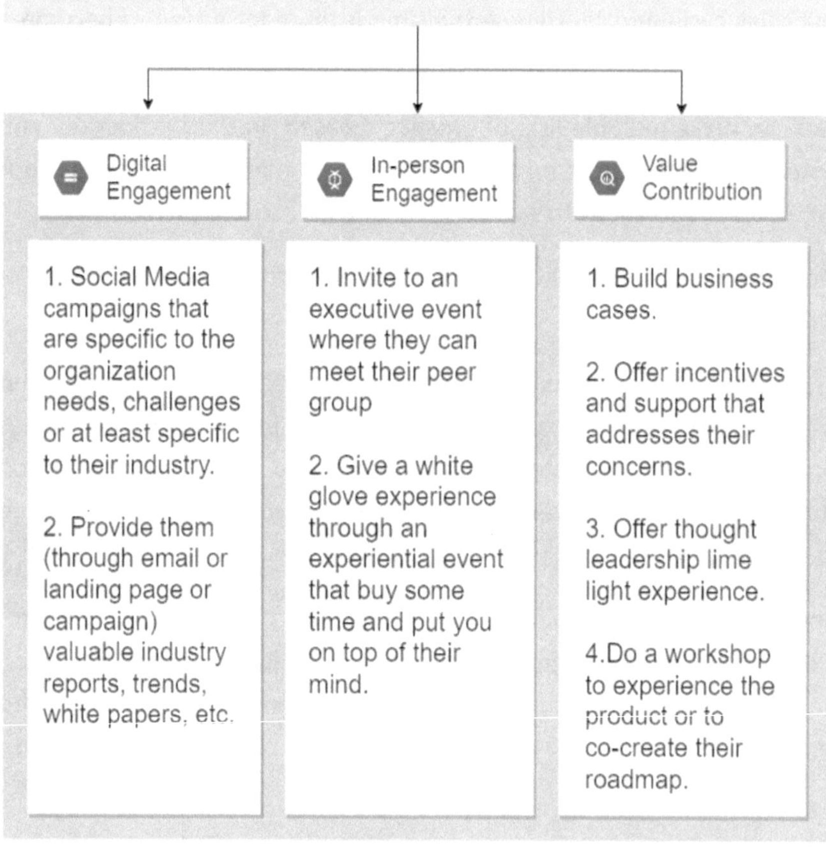

Tactic #11: Web Personalization using a deanonymizing tool

Stage of Funnel: TOFU   MOFU   BOFU

Channels Involved: Web

Tactic Description: Deanonymizing website visitors is the process of identifying anonymous website visitors and associating them with their organization's identity. This is an important process in Account-Based Marketing (ABM), as it allows marketers to personalize their marketing efforts and create more targeted campaigns. There are several ways that deanonymization can be achieved:

1. IP Address: One common way to deanonymize website visitors is to use their IP address to identify them. This can be done by comparing their IP address to a database of known IP addresses associated with specific companies or individuals.

2. Cookies: Another way to deanonymize website visitors is by using cookies. When a visitor lands on a website, a cookie is stored on their computer that contains information about their visit. By analyzing this cookie data, marketers can identify the visitor and personalize their experience.

3. Login Information: If a website requires visitors to log in to access certain content or features, this can be used to deanonymize them. By requiring visitors to provide personal information to create an account, marketers can identify and personalize their experience.

Some of the personalization tools are 6 Sense, Clearbit, Leadfeeder and Mutiny. While using this tactic, make sure that you're not violating any data privacy as per the country's norms. The typical match rates of these tools are 40 to 60%.

Example: A leading B2B EdTech company leveraged advanced IP address tracking tools and reverse IP lookup technology to identify the organizations visiting their website. By matching the IP addresses of the website visitors with public databases and proprietary sources, they could determine the companies behind the anonymous traffic.

The de-anonymization process was seamlessly integrated with the company's CRM and marketing automation systems. This enabled the marketing team to personalize and automate their communication based on the visitor's organization.

Execution Steps:

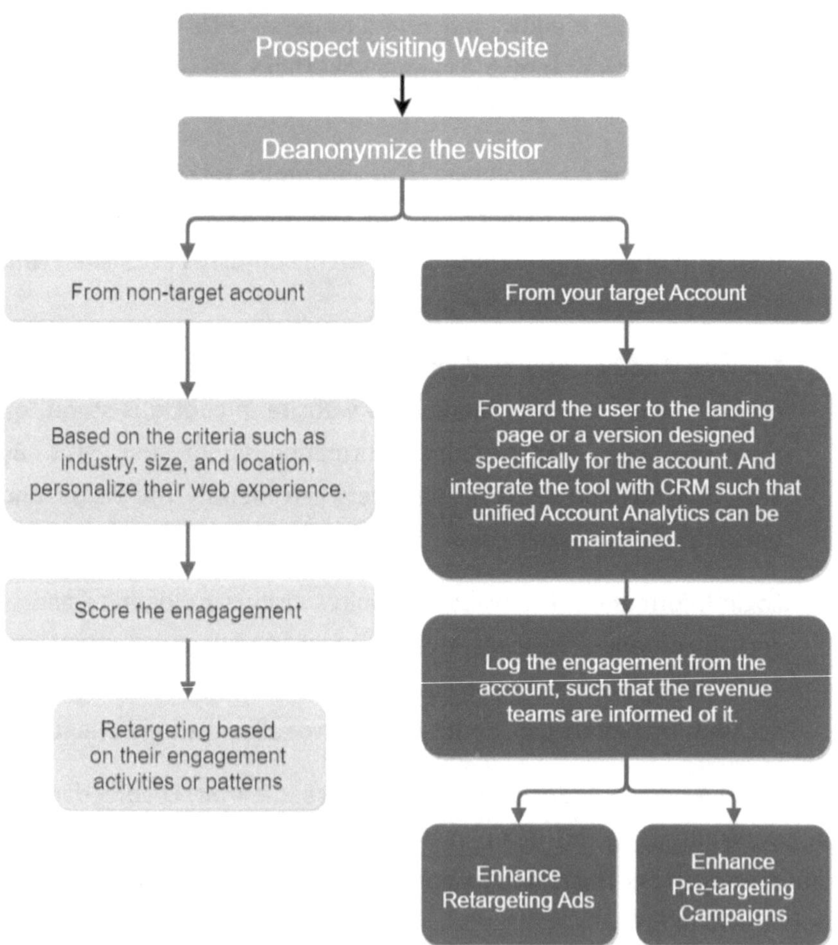

Tactic #12: Making Every Occasion Count - Gifting

Stage of Funnel: MOFU   BOFU

Channels Involved: Direct Mailer, Event

Tactic Description: This tactic gifting on the occasion of milestones in a prospect's professional journey or on specific occasions such as work anniversaries, religious festivals, and organization achievements.

This process demands alignment between your market research team, account management, marketing, sales, finance, and the vendors involved. Choose appropriate gifts that are personal and thoughtful but not offensive.

Some of the gifting options are:

1.   leaf art of their photo,

2.   personalized electronic items like earbuds with their name,

3.   artwork of their photo (caricature, canvas painting, etc.),

4.   Naming a star after them,

5.   Sand art,

6.   Flowers, Cake, Chocolates,

7.   A detailed journal of their professional journey

This ABM tactic of gifting can help build relationships with prospects and show that their business is valued.

P.S: Avoid gifting anything that is sexual in nature, racially offensive, suggests violence, or promotes unethical behaviour.

Example: A media agency celebrated its customer's achievement of reaching the $100M revenue milestone by sending them a specially designed cake. The cake was meticulously crafted to incorporate the customer's brand guidelines and included a congratulatory message.

This demonstrated their focus and inclination towards their customers' success.

Execution Steps:

Step 1 - Anchoring

Design your internal gifting process. This will include

1. Design the data fields that have to be captured before gifting anyone, data fields like their organization gifting policy, birthday, work anniversary, religious inclinations, expenditure affordability, Current engagement state (to avoid red flags), etc.

2. Curate a list of gift items while finalizing your vendor or multiple vendors.

3. Develop an automated process that will send the list to your vendor (like an e-commerce portal) and they will process this list for delivering the gift on the specific dates. The list needs to specify what has to be delivered to whom, to where and on what date.

Step 2 - Take off

Once the process is established:

1. Gather Information: Collect as much information as possible about your prospects including their birthday, work anniversary, religious inclination, sports inclination, successful implementation, organization's success, etc.

2. Before subscribing to a company's key stakeholders, make sure you're not going against any of their policies. For example, some companies may have strict policies against receiving gifts above a certain value or type of gifts.

3. Compliment this gifting process with an in-person visit or a phone call before or after.

Tactic #13: One stone, two birds - Dine & Wine event with a mix of customers and prospects

Stage of Funnel: TOFU   MOFU   BOFU

Channels Involved: Event

Tactic Description: The ABM tactic of doing a dinner event with a mix of customers and prospects is a great way to foster relationships and build connections between these groups, while also providing an opportunity to showcase your product or service in a more informal and relaxed setting.

The idea is to bring together a select group of customers and prospects in an intimate setting, such as a private dining room at a restaurant or a special event venue, for a night of networking with prospects and relationship-building with both customers.

Personalized hospitality, right from the invitation, to logistics, to welcoming at the venue, introducing the group, delivering seating and food experiences, and others, can keep you in the top memory lane of the prospect and customer mind.

The focus of the event should be on building relationships, not showcasing your product or service. Taking through a presentation is not at all advised.

Example: A B2B SaaS company organized a dinner event at an exclusive restaurant for their prospects in pipe (MOFU/BOFU) along with some of their best customers. To ensure a balanced mix, they maintained a 3:1 ratio between prospects and customers. The seating arrangement was strategically designed to ensure that each customer was easily accessible to at least two prospects.

Execution Steps:

Step 1: Identify the Right Mix

Identify the right mix of customers and prospects: The success of this tactic depends on inviting the right people. The guest list should be carefully curated to include a mix of existing customers and high-value prospects who are likely to benefit from meeting each other.

Prospects Cluster		Customers Cluster
CRITERIAS		ALL PROSPECTS CRITERIAS +
* Designation	* ICP Match %	+ Implementation Date
* Location	* Persona	+ Existing Relationship score
* Stage of deal	* Aspirations	+ Revenue Growth Opportunity
* Engagement Score	* Challenges	+ Satisfaction Score
* Pipe Value		+ Implemented Solutions (should match with the prospect's interested
* Industry		+ Willing to give Testimonial
* Interested in Solutions		+ Willing to leverage Thought Leadership opportunity
* Willingness to network		

Step 2: Choose the Right Venue

The venue should be chosen based on the number of guests, the type of event, and the budget. A private dining room at a high-end restaurant, a rooftop bar, or a unique event space are all great options.

Step 3: Plan the menu and sitting

Plan the menu: The menu should be carefully planned to accommodate any dietary restrictions and to provide a memorable dining experience. Consider working with the restaurant or catering company to customize the menu and make it special for your guests.

Plan the seating: Place name tags at each seat and consider assigning seats to help facilitate conversation. Create icebreaker activities or conversation starters to help guests get to know each other.

Step 4: Keep the loop going

Follow up after the event: After the dinner, make sure to follow up with each attendee individually to thank them for coming and to continue the conversation. This can include personalized emails or phone calls, sending personalized gifts, or scheduling follow-up meetings to discuss potential business opportunities.

<u>Tactic #14:</u> Connect & Grow together with Customers

<u>**Stage of Funnel:**</u>   BOFU

<u>**Channels Involved:**</u> Event

<u>**Tactic Description:**</u> A customer success summit or customer connect event is all about bringing together your existing customers to share their success stories, showcase their achievements, and provide valuable insights and feedback on your product or service. This event serves as a platform to strengthen your relationship with your customers and demonstrate your commitment to their success.

Objectives:

1.   Strengthening your relationships with your customers,

2.   Building brand loyalty, increasing customer retention rates, and

3.   Generating new business opportunities through customer referrals.

Possible formats for the event:

1.   Half-day or full-day conference

2.   Multi-day summit

3.   Hybrid (both online and face-to-face) event

4.   An interactive workshop

5.   A panel discussion

6.   Customer Advocacy Council meeting

7.   Award ceremony

The event can cover a range of topics, such as best practices for using your product or service, emerging trends in the industry, case studies from successful customers, and strategies for overcoming common business challenges. You can also invite guest speakers and thought leaders to share their insights and expertise on relevant topics.

Example: A leading B2B SaaS company organized a Customer Success Summit. This event was aimed at bringing together existing customers to create success stories, showcase achievements, and generate new business opportunities.

The Customer Success Summit spanned two days and included entertainment activities, rewarding quizzes, keynote presentations, customer success stories, interactive workshops, panel discussions, customer advocacy meetings and an award ceremony.

Execution Steps:

Step 1: Craft the Criteria

Design a scoring formula to segment and prioritize customers that to be invited to the event. The parameters could be ACV, CSAT, location, opportunity value, industry, and their Success Story, etc.

Step 2: Upkeep the List

Keep maintaining your customer list updated from time to time. Your list size could signal you the time for an event like Customer connect, Customer Success, etc.

Step 3: Design the format

Based on the list of customers you want to invite, design a plan with a mix of presentations, panel discussions, breakout sessions, customer advocacy board meeting, etc.

Step 4: Event Activities

Design the event with ample time for networking and socializing, so customers can connect with each other and with your team. You can host a cocktail hour, a dinner, a TV studio set up for thought leadership videos and other activities for relationship-building.

Step 5: Keep up the momentum

After the event, follow up with attendees to thank them for coming, provide any additional resources or information, and ask for feedback on how you can improve for next time.

Tactic #15: Social Listening + Semantic Analytics = Intent

Stage of Funnel: TOFU   MOFU   BOFU

Channels Involved: Martech

Tactic Description: This ABM tactic involves using automatic social listening, deep sentiment analysis, and semantic analytics. Use technology to monitor social media and other online platforms for mentions of your brand and related keywords, and then analyze the sentiment and meaning behind these mentions.

The idea is to gather information about your target accounts and their pain points, interests, and preferences by analyzing their social media activity. This information can then be used to personalize your ABM campaigns and messaging.

Automatic social listening involves setting up automated processes to monitor social media platforms, such as Twitter, LinkedIn, Facebook, and Instagram, for posts from your target accounts. These posts can be further analyzed to keep you informed about the journey of your account and decode their communication tone.

Semantic analytics, on the other hand, is a more complex technique that involves analyzing the meaning of language and the relationships between words and phrases. This type of analysis goes beyond just looking at the sentiment of a post and instead focuses on the underlying meaning of the language used. By using semantic analytics, companies can gain a deeper understanding of the topics, themes, and concepts that are being discussed by customers and prospects on social media and other online channels.

Execution Steps:

Step 1: Set up Tools & Channels to be monitored

Choose the list of accounts that you want to listen to various platforms. Use tools to listen to their social media, websites, press releases, blog, video channels, annual/quarterly report etc.

Step 2: Gather the Data

Gather the data from various sources in various formats and unify them along with the data from other account intelligence tools. Drive your data into your repositories such as CRM, ABM tools and others.

Step 3: Insights Gathering

By using semantic analytics, gain a deeper understanding of the topics, themes, and concepts that are being discussed by the accounts and prospects. You can also decode their choice of words and tone of their voice to communicate back.

Step 4: Embed insights into communications

Use the insights to get a real-time understanding of customer and prospect, identify opportunities, engage with them and quickly respond to issues or opportunities as they arise. Make use of identified trends and insights that can be used in communication.

Step 5: Keep the Engine Running

Keep iterating the process of gathering data, analysis, embedding the insights in communications and enabling your revenue teams. Refine your engine with respect to its sources of data, algorithm of analyzing and ways of using insights.

Tactic #16: Customer Advisory Council for ABM Success

Stage of Funnel: BOFU

Channels Involved: In-person meet and Event

Tactic Description: The customer advisory council involves creating a forum for open dialogue with executives of key customers. The purpose of this council is to gain a better understanding of the customer's objectives, challenges, and what is holding them back and to provide guidance.

The council should be formed of influential individuals who can provide insights and feedback on the company's products or services. The meetings are held according to Chatham House Rules, which allow the participants to have an open and honest discussion without fear of information being shared outside the group.

The information gathered from these meetings can be used to inform the company's ABM strategy, such as creating targeted marketing messages or developing new products and services that meet the specific needs of the customers.

Involving customers in the process demonstrates that their feedback is valued, and your organization can create a sense of partnership with the customers.

Example: An MNC IT company has run 10 global boards with 100 members. These customer advisory boards help customers in understanding their unique needs and addressing them with solutions. In return, the company has received feedback and insights for its products and services that help them in the evolution of their product and designing their roadmap.

The meetings ensure confidentiality and encourage participants to freely share their opinions, challenges, and aspirations. The company carefully selected influential individuals from their key customers to form the Customer Advisory Council. These individuals were chosen based on their industry expertise, influence within their organizations, and their ability to provide valuable insights and feedback.

Execution Steps:

Step 1 - Identify Accounts: Identify the most important customers that you want to engage in a customer advisory council. These customers should be strategic to your business and represent a diverse group of industries and geographies.

Step 2 - Invite customers: Reach out to these customers and invite them to participate in a customer advisory council. Explain the purpose of the council and what they can expect from participating.

Step 3 - Schedule meetings: Schedule regular meetings with the customer advisory council members. These meetings should be held in-person or virtually and should be conducted with Chatham House rules to encourage open and honest dialogue.

Step 4 - Discuss objectives and challenges: Use these meetings to discuss the customer's objectives and challenges. This will help you understand their goals and how you can help them.

Step 5 - Provide input: Use the feedback and insights from the customer advisory council meetings to inform your ABM strategy. This will help you create personalized experiences and solutions for your customers.

Step 6 - Follow up: After each meeting, follow up with the customers to provide any additional information or resources that they need. This will help you build strong relationships and show them that you are committed to their success..

Tactic #17: Collaborative Workshops with Customers

Stage of Funnel:　　BOFU

Channels Involved: Event

Tactic Description: This tactic intends to empower customers through your products and services. The enabled customer will, in turn, help with referrals and become your brand advocate.

Example: An IOT company has invited its customers from Manufacturing Industry to demonstrate the value its product and services can deliver to the organizations. These workshops were aimed at generating ideas, brainstorming solutions, and co-creating innovative solutions.

The workshops provided a platform for customers to share their expertise, perspectives, and expectations while fostering an environment of open dialogue and creative thinking. The company has invited both engineers and executives to display the technical and business value perspectives. This workshop included hands-on, brainstorming and feedback sessions.

The company facilitated the workshops with a team of experts who specialized in product development, design thinking, and customer experience. These facilitators guided the discussions, encouraged active participation, and ensured that the workshops remained focused on achieving actionable outcomes.

During the workshops, the company encouraged rapid prototyping of ideas and concepts. Customers had the opportunity to provide immediate feedback on prototypes, allowing for iterative improvements and ensuring that the final solutions aligned closely with their needs and expectations. By hosting these workshops, the company achieved stronger customer relationships, insights, improved product & service alignment, and thought leadership.

Execution Steps:

Step 1

Set the agenda of the workshop

Choose the venue and format of the workshop

This can be multiday event depending up on who are being addressed in the key stakeholders and how many days would they need to be enabled.

Develop the content for all the stakeholders including end users, managers, and the leadership team to be presented in the workshop. The content should be engaging, informative, and provide practical knowledge.

Content that bespeaks the best practices and the ways to monitor its utilization while ensuring the best customer support from you

Step 2

Empower decision makers and leadership team with data or roadmap through TCOs or the business outcomes that they have achieved so far and what can they do going further

Enable Users to make the full utilization of your products & services with the best sources available readily for them to learn or to implement.

You can cover include Technical topics, Hands-on sessions, Panel discussions, gamified sessions, contests, certifications, etc.

Facilitate the sessions, ensuring that they are engaging and that attendees are able to ask questions and participate in discussions.

After the workshop, gather feedback from attendees on what they liked and what could be improved. Use this feedback to improve future workshops.

Tactic #18: Making the Prospect's visit memorable - personalized hospitality

Stage of Funnel: BOFU

Channels Involved: In-person meet

Tactic Description: This ABM tactic is all about creating a personalized and memorable experience for a key prospect who is visiting your office. This can also happen after the invitation to a tender while the evaluation process is in progress.

Example: A prospect was visiting India as part of the process of evaluating the top 3 companies competing for a tender. A small company, being an underdog, took the best out of this opportunity through this tactic. The company has carefully crafted a memorable experience for the visitor. The plan was detailed right from welcoming him at the reception to giving him an office tour.

They even allocated a dedicated office, tastefully decorated to reflect what it would be like to collaborate with them. The decoration theme was thoughtfully aligned with the visitor's organization's culture, adding a personalized touch to the experience.

Execution Steps:

Step 1

Research the prospect: Before the prospect arrives, do thorough research on them and their company culture, vision, values, products, company policies, etc. This will help you understand their preferences and what they might like to see or experience during their visit.

Step 2

Design the workspace: Once you have a good understanding of the prospect's company culture, design the workspace in a way that reflects their values and vision. This could include customizing the decor, displaying relevant materials, and incorporating elements that align with their brand.

Step 3

Create customized content: To further personalize the experience, create content in different formats that aligns with the prospect's viewpoints and interests. This could include a customized presentation, video, or even a slide show.

Provide personalized hospitality: During the visit, provide personalized hospitality that exceeds their expectations. This could include a customized welcome package, a personalized tour of the facility, and meals or snacks that reflect their personal preferences.

Step 4

Give a personalized gift: As a parting gesture, give the prospect a personalized gift that aligns with their CSR activities or personal interests, without breaking their company policies.

Tactic #19: Innovation Workshop with Prospect

Stage of Funnel: MOFU   BOFU

Channels Involved: In-person meet and Event.

Tactic Description: This tactic involves bringing together key stakeholders from the prospective company to work on a mutually beneficial business outcome.

Example: A Telecom company organized an innovation workshop with its e-commerce prospects to demonstrate its new technology. The workshop aimed to demonstrate the technology's ability to deliver new-age customer experiences. The event included a hands-on session along with a panel discussion featuring telecom and e-commerce experts.

Execution Steps:

Step 1	Step 2	Step 3
Gather Account Insights	**Analyze Insights**	**Develop value added propositions**
* Gather account insights: Start by gathering all the relevant information about the prospect account. This includes their business goals, objectives, pain points, and challenges. * Use this information to understand their unique business needs and requirements.	* Once you have gathered all the account insights, analyze them to identify the key areas where you can add value. * This will help you identify the opportunities for innovation and collaboration.	* Based on the account insights and analysis, develop value-added propositions that address the key challenges and pain points of the prospect. * These propositions should align with the prospect's business goals and objectives.

Step 4

Organize the workshop

* Invite the key stakeholders from the prospect company to participate in the workshop.

* The workshop should be designed to be interactive and collaborative, with a focus on achieving a shared vision and goals.

Step 5

Share Insights

* Start the workshop by sharing the insights gathered during the ground work.

* This will help the participants gain a deeper understanding of the issues being faced by the prospect and set the stage for collaboration.

Step 6

Prioritize ideas and solutions

* Encourage the participants to share their ideas and solutions to the challenges being faced by the prospect.

* Prioritize the ideas and solutions based on their potential impact and feasibility.

Step 7

Conclude on objectives, goals, journey, and metrics

* Work together with the participants to define the objectives, goals, journey, and metrics for the collaboration.

* This will help ensure that everyone is aligned and committed to achieving the desired outcomes.

Step 8

Co-create a roadmap & Action plan

* Use the insights gathered during the workshop to co-create a roadmap or plan for achieving the objectives and goals.

* The roadmap should include key milestones, timelines, and DRIs (Directly Responsible Individuals).

Tactic #20: ABM with Funnel Building through Content Syndication

Stage of Funnel: TOFU

Channels Involved: 3rd party Web

Tactic Description: Content syndication is the process of promoting content across different channels or platforms to reach a wider audience. In ABM, content syndication is used to reach potential customers with targeted and relevant content that addresses their specific pain points and challenges.

Execution Steps:

Step 1: Create high-quality content that is tailored to your target accounts. This content can be in the form of whitepapers, case studies, research reports, or any other format that provides value to your target accounts. The content should also include qualifying questions that help identify prospects who are interested in your solution and are worth pursuing.

Step 2: Once the content is created, the next step is to syndicate it across different channels or platforms that your target accounts frequent. This can include social media platforms, industry publications, or other websites where your target accounts are likely to spend time. By syndicating the content, you can increase the reach of your message and drive more traffic to your website.

Step 3: After the initial touch points through content syndication, the next step is to invite qualified prospects to a virtual or face-to-face event. This event can be a webinar, a roundtable discussion, or any other format that allows for a deeper engagement with your target accounts. During the event, you can share more insights and information about your solution, and provide opportunities for prospects to ask questions and interact with your team.

<u>Tactic #21</u>: Reward-Based Interviews with ICP Prospects on a functional basis

<u>**Stage of Funnel:**</u>   TOFU

<u>**Channels Involved:**</u> Online Meet, In-person meet and Focus Groups

<u>**Tactic Description:**</u> The ABM tactic of interviewing ICP prospects and offering them rewards is a great way to gather valuable information about the prospects and their decision-making processes. This information can then be used to tailor your ABM strategy to better meet the needs of your target audience.

Execution Steps:

<u>Step 1</u>: Identify the Ideal Customer Profile (ICP) prospects you want to target and approach them with an invitation to participate in the interview.

Be clear about the reward they will receive in exchange for their time and insights.

<u>Step 2</u>: Prepare a list of questions for interview that will help you understand the prospect's buying criteria, touchpoints, sources of information, challenges, KRAs, KPIs, and decision-making processes. Make sure the questions are open-ended and allow the prospect to provide detailed answers.

<u>Step 3</u>: After the interview, analyze the data collected and use it to inform your ABM strategy.

Identify areas where your product or service can meet the prospect's needs. With the first few responses validated you can

<u>Step 4</u>: Finally, send the reward to the prospect as a thank-you for their participation.

This could be in the form of a gift card, voucher, or other token of appreciation.

Tactic #22: Reward-Based Perception Interviews with Customers

Stage of Funnel: BOFU

Channels Involved: Online Meet and In-person meet

Tactic Description: Conducting a perception interview with customers is an ABM tactic that involves gathering insights and feedback from existing customers about their perceptions and experiences with your product or service. This approach can help you identify areas where you need to improve, understand what customers value most, and gather insights that can be used to inform your account-based marketing strategy.

Example: A SAAS company conducted its Perception interview with all its customers while aiming for retention and capturing insights on their products and services. The company offered $100 for their 15 minutes of time over a call. These interviews helped not only capture insights and suggestions on their products and services but also strengthened their relationship with the customers.

Execution Steps:

Step 1: Define the objective: Identify the specific objective you want to achieve through the perception interview. For example, you may want to understand how customers perceive your product or service, what challenges they face, or how you can improve your customer experience.

Step 2: Identify the right customers: Select the customers you want to interview based on their relevance to the objective. It is recommended to select a mix of happy and dissatisfied customers, as this can provide a balanced perspective.

 **Step 3: Prepare the questions:** Develop a set of open-ended questions that align with your objective. Questions should be designed to elicit detailed and thoughtful responses.

 **Step 4: Conduct the interview:** Schedule the interview with the selected customers and conduct the interview. Encourage customers to speak freely and openly about their experiences.

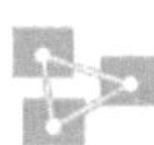 **Step 5: Record and analyze the responses:** Record the responses of the customers in a structured manner. Analyze the responses to identify common themes, insights, and patterns. These insights can help you understand the needs, preferences, and expectations of your customers.

 **Step 6: Develop action plans:** Based on the insights gained from the perception interviews, develop action plans to address customer needs and improve the customer experience.

 **Step 7: Share the results:** Share the results of the perception interviews with relevant stakeholders across your organization, such as marketing, sales, product, and customer support. This can help create a customer-centric culture and drive customer loyalty and advocacy.

 **Step 8: Follow-up:** Follow up with the interviewed customers to show that their feedback is valued, and to keep them engaged with your brand. Consider offering incentives or discounts to encourage continued engagement.

Tactic #23: Celebrating Customer Success with Personalized Gifting

Stage of Funnel: BOFU

Channels Involved: Direct Mailer

Tactic Description: Celebrating your customer's success is a great way to build a strong relationship with them and show that you care about their business. The goal of this ABM tactic is to show your customers that you care about their success. By taking the time to celebrate their achievements, you can build a strong foundation for a long-lasting relationship.

Execution Steps:

<u>Tactic #24:</u> Strategic Tender Pursuit Campaign with ABM

<u>Stage of Funnel:</u>   BOFU   MOFU

<u>Channels Involved:</u> In-person meet

<u>Tactic Description:</u> This ABM tactic involves a strategic approach to winning a tender deal.

Execution Steps:

Step 1 — Thorough research: Conduct thorough research on the organization you're pursuing and its stakeholders, including their goals, challenges, and pain points. Analyze their current solutions and identify areas of improvement while understanding the Tender process in completely.

Step 2 — Identify key influencers: Understand their buying process, priorities, needs, concerns, and identify key decision-makers and influencers within the organization. This will help in designing targeted messaging and campaigns.

Step 3 — Design value proposition: Develop value propositions that promise to meet the organization's goals and challenges. This should include associated technical solutions that align with their existing roadmap.

Step 4 — Enable sales teams: Enable sales teams at all stages of the bidding process through strategic and tactical campaigns based on the changing priorities of the customer. This will ensure that the messaging is tailored to their specific needs and concerns.

Step 5 — Analyze feedback: Analyze the feedback and analytics of the campaign and discussions with the customer. This will provide insights into the effectiveness of the messaging and value propositions and inform the next campaign, messaging, and value propositions.

Tactic #25: Gamifying ABM - Rewarding Your Team

Stage of Funnel: TOFU   MOFU   BOFU

Channels Involved: Channel agnostic

Tactic Description: Gamifying an ABM program internally can be an effective way to motivate and reward your ABM team for their success.

Metrics to Measure/Reward: Number of Calls, number of accounts penetrated, number of key stakeholders per account engaged, number of meetings, value of pipe, value of closure, etc.

Execution Steps:

Step 1

Define clear objectives:

Before designing the game mechanics, define clear objectives for your ABM program and its scoring mechanism.

Step 2

Design a point system:

Create a point system that rewards your team members for achieving specific ABM milestones, such as securing a meeting with a key decision-maker or closing a deal with a high-value account. Assign point values to each milestone and track them in a leaderboard that is visible to the entire team.

Step 3

Set up challenges:

Create challenges that encourage your team members to work together to achieve specific goals. For example, you could set up a challenge to see which team can secure the most meetings with high-value accounts in a given month. Monitor the progress of your ABM program and adjust the game as needed.

Step 4

Offer rewards:

Offer rewards for achieving specific milestones or winning challenges. These rewards can be as simple as gift cards or as complex as trips or other experiential rewards.

Tactic #26: A Strategic Approach to Win Big Deals

Stage of Funnel: MOFU   BOFU

Channels Involved: Channel agnostic

Tactic Description: By applying the ABM approach to major sales opportunities in the pipeline, you can increase your chances of success.

Execution Steps:

Demand Generation or Inbound here: Identify the lead generated with high potential to be well navigated.

ABM Program Starts here   Lead

Include the generated lead into the ABM program

ABM Step1: Gather insights & Build Team: Conduct thorough research to gather insights about the account, including their business challenges, priorities, and decision-making processes. This will help you tailor your messaging and approach to their specific needs. Assemble a cross-functional team that includes sales, marketing, and other relevant stakeholders to work on the opportunity.

ABM Step2: Develop a customized plan: Based on the insights gathered, develop a customized plan that includes targeted messaging, content, and tactics designed to engage the account and move them through the sales funnel. This may include customized events, webinars, and other tactics designed specifically for the account.

ABM Step3: Execute the plan: With the plan in place, it's time to execute. This should be a coordinated effort across the cross-functional team.

ABM Step4: Measure and optimize: Measure the effectiveness of the plan and optimize as needed. This may involve adjusting tactics based on feedback from the account or refining messaging based on engagement metrics.

<u>Tactic #27:</u> Building an internal ABM community.

<u>Stage of Funnel:</u>   TOFU   MOFU   BOFU

<u>Channels Involved:</u> Martech, Events.

<u>Tactic Description:</u> Building an internal ABM community is a great way to keep your employees and partners involved in your ABM program. By creating a dedicated community, you can foster collaboration, encourage knowledge sharing, and provide ongoing education and training opportunities to help your team stay up-to-date on the latest trends and best practices.

<u>Example:</u> A global technology company established a dedicated community platform where employees and partners could connect, collaborate, and share insights related to ABM. This platform served as a centralized hub for discussions, resource sharing, and learning opportunities.

The company organized regular training sessions, webinars, and workshops focused on ABM best practices, industry trends, and relevant skill development. They also showcased success stories and case studies from their ABM initiatives within the community.

The company implemented a system to recognize and reward active contributors within the ABM community. They acknowledged individuals who shared valuable insights, provided helpful guidance, or contributed to the overall knowledge base. This recognition was in the form of certificates, badges, or other incentives.

Execution Steps:

Step 1:
Build the
team

Step 2:
Set Goals,
processes

Start by identifying your key stakeholders who should be involved in the community. This may include your marketing, sales, and customer success teams, as well as any partners or vendors.

Next, establish clear goals and objectives for the community. This might include sharing best practices, discussing industry trends, or providing training and education on ABM-related topics.

Step 3:
The
Platform

Choose a platform for the community, such as a private social network or a dedicated Slack channel. Make sure the platform is easy to use and accessible to all members of the community.

Step 4:
Interact
Frequently

Step 5:
Upskill &
Synergize

Set up regular meetings for the community, such as monthly or quarterly webinars or in-person meetups. Use these meetings to share updates, discuss challenges, and collaborate on new ideas.

Offer ongoing education and training opportunities to help members of the community stay up-to-date on the latest ABM trends and best practices. This might include webinars, workshops, or online courses.

Tactic #28: Utilizing Contract Database Trackers

Stage of Funnel: TOFU   MOFU

Channels Involved: Martech

Tactic Description: This tactic is about using contract database trackers to gain insights into the contract details of target accounts. These tools, provided by agencies such as IDC, ISG, and Ovum from OMDIA, can provide a list of contracts, their status, deal size, contractors, and other details that can help inform an ABM strategy.

Execution Steps:

Step 1: Need for a contract database tracker:

Assess your organization's need for a contract database tracker by evaluating the current processes for tracking contracts, identifying any pain points, and determining the potential benefits of using a dedicated tracker.

Step 2: Identify vendors:

Research vendors that offer contract database trackers. Some popular vendors include IDC, ISG, and Ovum from OMDIA. Consider factors such as the vendor's reputation, the range of features offered, and the cost of the service.

Step 3: Set up the contract database tracker:

Once you've chosen the vendor, set up the contract database tracker. This may involve configuring the system to meet your specific requirements and training users on how to use the system.

Step 4: Integrate the tracker

Once the tracker is set up, use the insights gained from the contract database tracker to inform your ABM program. For example, use data on contract size and status to target accounts that are most likely to yield high-value opportunities.

Step 5: Continuously evaluate and refine

Regularly evaluate the effectiveness of your contract database tracker and refine your processes as needed. This may involve gathering feedback from users, monitoring key performance metrics, and identifying opportunities for further optimization.

Tactic #29: Social Media Selling

Stage of Funnel: TOFU   MOFU

Channels Involved: Social Media, Web and Paid Media

Tactic Description: This tactic involves leveraging social media platforms like LinkedIn, Twitter, and Instagram to engage with decision-makers and influencers at target accounts and build relationships with them.

Example: A VR & AR company that specializes in creating immersive experiences for the real estate and fashion industries has harnessed the power of social media. They strategically curated a list of audiences based on their ICP (Ideal Customer Profile) and personas on platforms like LinkedIn and Instagram.

They ran advertising campaigns to find out what messages were attracting their target segments. Through split-testing, they identified the messages that resonated the most with their audience. As a result, they developed verified and high-performing value propositions and messages. These compelling value propositions and messages are utilized in their interactions with prospects.

Having the right target audience on Linkedin, right messages and right value propositions they started outreaching on Linkedin through connection requests, message requests and Inmails.

Execution Steps:

Step 1

PROCESS

Identify your target accounts and key decision makers. Use data and insights to identify the companies and individuals you want to engage with on social media.

Step 2

RESEARCH

Research your prospects - Learn more about your prospects by reviewing their social media profiles and understanding their interests, challenges, and pain points.

Step 3

PERSONALIZATION

Develop customized content that addresses your prospects' needs and interests. This could include blog posts, infographics, videos, or other types of content.

Step 4

SOCIAL MEDIA

Use social media to like, comment on, and share your prospects' posts. This will help build a relationship and establish your company as a thought leader in their industry.

Step 5

ADVERTISING

Leverage social media advertising. Use targeted social media advertising to reach your prospects and promote your content and brand.

Step 6

MEASURE

Monitor your social media campaigns and track key metrics like engagement, clicks, and conversions. Use this data to optimize your campaigns and improve your results over time.

<u>Tactic #30:</u> Thought Leadership Podcasting

<u>Stage of Funnel:</u>   MOFU   BOFU

<u>Channels Involved:</u> Podcast and Social Media

<u>Tactic Description:</u> Creating a podcast episode specific to the challenges or opportunities of a target account is an effective way to establish thought leadership in their industry and show that you understand the specific context or problem they are facing.

<u>Example:</u> A Cyber security company has sponsored a season of a popular podcast that voices the cyber security industry. To strategically target potential enterprise organizations, the company compiled a list of key accounts they aimed to penetrate. They extended invitations to the key decision-makers from these potential accounts.

The podcast was hosted by an industry subject matter expert (SME) and featured discussions involving both the prospects and the SME from the sponsoring company. Following the publication of each podcast episode, the company actively promoted them, ensuring the establishment of thought leadership for both the company and the prospect.

Through this sponsorship and podcast collaboration, the cyber security company effectively leveraged the podcast's reach and engaged key decision-makers within the target accounts, positioning themselves as thought leaders in the industry and fostering valuable connections with potential clients.

Execution Steps:

1. Identify the Target Accounts

The first step is to identify the specific target account that you want to focus on. This could be a current or potential customer that you want to engage with.

2. Research the Account

Once you have identified the target account, research their industry, business, and challenges. Use social media, news articles, and other sources to gather as much information as possible.

3. Challenges & Opportunities

Based on your research, identify the specific challenges or opportunities that the target account is facing. These could be related to their industry, business goals, or other factors.

4. Podcast Execution

You can have your own podcast or sponsor a podcast series. Use the insights gathered in the previous steps to plan the podcast episode. Determine the topic, format, and guests for the episode. Consider what insights or expertise you can provide that will be of value to the target account.

5. Invite

If you plan to have guests on the podcast, reach out to them and invite them to participate. Be clear about the topic and format of the episode and what you hope to achieve.

6. Promote

Once the episode is produced, promote it to the target account and their industry. Share it on social media, post it on your website, and send it directly to the target account. Consider running targeted ads or social media campaigns to reach a wider audience

Tactic #31: Customized Landing Pages for Accounts

Stage of Funnel: TOFU   MOFU

Channels Involved: Web, Paid Media, Social Media and Martech.

Tactic Description: The ABM tactic of creating customized landing pages for accounts is an effective way to show your commitment and value proposition to the account even before they commit to working with you. By personalizing your messaging and tailoring your solutions to their specific needs, you can increase your chances of winning their business.

Execution Steps:

Step 1: Identify the Accounts

First, identify the high-value accounts that you want to target with this tactic. These accounts should have a high potential for revenue and be a good fit for your business.

Step 2: Gather Account Insights

Once you have identified the accounts, gather as much information as possible about their business, challenges, and goals. This will help you create a personalized landing page that speaks directly to their needs.

Step 3: Create the Landing Page

Create a landing page that includes information about your company's solutions, how they align with the account's needs personalize messaging that speaks directly to the account and using their company name and industry-specific language. Also ensure that that landing page is not indexed by Google.

Step 4: Share the Landing Page

Once the landing page is created, share it with the account through email or other communication channels. Be sure to explain why you created the landing page and how it can help them achieve their goals.

Step 5: Track & Monitor

Use website analytics to track engagement with the landing page. Use screen recordings, heatmaps & URL parameters to track the visits and engagement patterns.

Tactic #32: Celebrity-driven ABM Events

Stage of Funnel: MOFU   BOFU

Channels Involved: Event

Tactic Description: The use of celebrities can help add an extra level of intrigue and excitement to events, as well as increase attendance and engagement among your target accounts. Depending on the nature of the event and the preferences of your target accounts, you may choose to work with a range of different types of celebrities, such as musicians, actors, athletes, or industry experts.

Example: A cybersecurity organization hosted an annual industry conference with the goal of bringing together professionals, industry leaders, and decision-makers in the security space.

To make the event even more impactful, they incorporated a well-known technology celebrity, who was recognized as a visionary entrepreneur and a leading expert in cyber security technologies.

The celebrity, who is a highly respected figure in the cybersecurity industry, had a distinguished career as a former hacker turned cybersecurity consultant. She was known for her extensive knowledge, expertise, and ability to demystify complex security concepts for both technical and non-technical audiences. Leveraging her reputation and influence, the B2B cybersecurity technology company invited her to be the keynote speaker at the summit.

She conducted an exclusive hands-on workshop that provided attendees with practical insights on securing their networks, identifying vulnerabilities, and implementing effective cybersecurity measures. Participants had the chance to interact directly with her, seeking guidance tailored to their specific organizational needs and challenges.

Execution Steps:

1 Identify Key Accounts

As with any ABM program, it is essential to identify the accounts that are most valuable to your business and to focus your efforts on engaging with these accounts.

2 Identify Celebrity

Research and identify well-known public figures who align with your brand values and who may be interested in partnering with your company for an event

3 Plan the event

Work with your celebrity partner to create a plan for the event that will resonate with your target accounts. This may involve choosing a theme, selecting a venue, and planning entertainment and other activities.

4 Customize Invitations

Develop customized invitations for each of your target accounts, highlighting the unique value that your event will offer the presence of the celebrity partner.

5 Share the Content

After the event, be sure to follow up with attendees to gather feedback and continue building relationships with your target accounts.

Tactic #33: Content Toolkit Centralization for ABM Reusability

Stage of Funnel: TOFU   MOFU   BOFU

Channels Involved: Web

Tactic Description: By developing a central toolkit, you can streamline your ABM efforts by ensuring that your team has access to the content and other assets the ABM program needs.

Execution Steps:

Step 1

Identify the content and assets: Start by identifying all the content and assets that your marketing and sales teams use during their ABM activities. This could include case studies, whitepapers, brochures, presentation decks, videos, and more.

Step 2

Organize the content: Once you have identified the content and assets, organize them in a central location that is easily accessible to everyone on the team. This could be a shared drive, a cloud-based platform, or a custom-built portal.

Step 3

Categorize the content: Categorize the content based on the type of asset, the stage of the buyer's journey, the vertical or industry, and any other relevant criteria. This will make it easier for team members to find and use the content they need for specific accounts.

Step 5

Develop templates: Develop templates for commonly used assets, such as presentations, email templates, and proposals. These templates should be customizable, allowing team members to tailor them to the specific needs of each account.

Step 5

Update the content regularly: Keep the content up to-date and relevant by regularly reviewing and updating it. This will ensure that the team is always using the latest and most accurate information when engaging with accounts.

Tactic #34: Dashboard for Data-driven approach

Stage of Funnel: TOFU   MOFU   BOFU

Channels Involved: Martech

Tactic Description: Having dashboard analytics for your ABM approach is an essential tool for measuring the success and effectiveness of your ABM program at both program and account levels.

The dashboard analytics should be easy to access and use, with real-time updates and customizable reporting options. This will enable your ABM team to make data-driven decisions, optimize their strategies, and identify areas for improvement.

Execution Steps:

Step 1: At Program Level

The dashboard analytics should provide an overview of the key performance indicators (KPIs) that are aligned with your ABM program's objectives. This could include metrics such as overall engagement levels, pipeline growth, revenue generated from ABM accounts, and ROI on your ABM investment.

The dashboard should also provide insights into the performance of your marketing channels and tactics, such as email campaigns, events, and content marketing.

Step 2: At Account Level

At the account level, the dashboard should provide detailed insights into the performance of individual accounts. including metrics such as account engagement, account growth potential, and deal velocity.

It should also provide insights into the account's key decision-makers, their interests, and engagement levels with your content and messaging.

Tactic #35: Account Prioritization for ABM Optimization

Stage of Funnel: TOFU

Channels Involved: Channel agnostic

Tactic Description: Develop a model for prioritizing accounts based on certain criteria, such as engagement score, fit with your Ideal Customer Profile, growth opportunity, and other factors that are specific to your business.

By prioritizing your accounts in this way, you can ensure that your sales and marketing teams are targeting the right prospects, delivering the right messages, and making the most of your resources.

Example: A technology company specialized in cloud-based solutions wanted to optimize their sales and marketing efforts by targeting the most valuable prospects. They developed a model for prioritizing accounts based on specific criteria tailored to their business.

The company identified the key criteria for prioritizing accounts. This included factors such as engagement score, fit with their Ideal Customer Profile (ICP), growth opportunity, revenue potential, industry alignment, and strategic alignment with their product offerings. They also considered factors unique to their business, such as customer acquisition costs and customer lifetime value.

This approach ensured that they allocated their resources wisely, targeted the right accounts with personalized messages, and maximized their revenue potential. The prioritization model provided a systematic framework for decision-making and allowed the company to make the most of its sales and marketing efforts.

Execution Steps:

Step 1: Define your Ideal Customer Profile (ICP): Start by creating a clear and detailed definition of your ICP based on factors such as company size, revenue potential, engagement scoreindustry, budget, decision-making process, and growth opportunity. Consider the top 20% of customers contributing your majority revenue, to derive the ICP genome. This way you can identify the accounts that are the best fit for your business.

Step 2: Assign weights to each criterion: Once you have defined your criteria, assign a weight to each one based on its importance to your business. This will help you calculate an overall score for each account and prioritize them accordingly.

Step 3: Score your accounts: Use your criteria and weighted scoring system to score each account in your target market. This will help you identify the accounts that are the highest priority for your business.

Step 4: Allocate resources: Based on your prioritized account list, allocate your resources (such as sales and marketing teams, budget, and time) to focus on the accounts that are most likely to generate revenue and provide long-term value to your business.

Step 5: Review and adjust your model: Regularly review and adjust your account prioritization model based on new data, feedback from your teams, and changes in your business strategy and goals.

Tactic #36: Combo Strategy with ABM & Vertical Marketing

Stage of Funnel: TOFU

Channels Involved: Channel agnostic

Tactic Description: The ABM tactic of collaborating with vertical marketing is all about bringing together the targeted and personalized approach of ABM with the industry-specific knowledge and expertise of vertical marketing. This tactic involves creating a cross-functional team that includes members from both ABM and vertical marketing and working together to develop a unified strategy that leverages the strengths of both approaches.

Example: A software company specialized in supply chain management solutions wanted to leverage their industry-specific knowledge and expertise. They collaborated on ABM with their vertical marketing team to create a unified strategy.

The company formed a cross-functional team with members from both the ABM and vertical marketing teams. While the ABM team orchestrated the customer journey, the vertical marketing team helped through insights, content and decision-making evaluations.

The team executed the collaborative strategy by implementing personalized campaigns, engaging with key decision-makers in the target accounts, and delivering industry-specific content and resources at scale.

This helped the company establish itself as an industry expert and build stronger relationships with its manufacturing and logistics customers.

Execution Steps:

Step 1: Identify Key Verticals : The first step is to identify the industry verticals that are most important to your business, and that would benefit from a targeted ABM approach. This might involve looking at factors like revenue potential, growth rates, market size and customer needs.

Step 2: Building Cross-functional Team: Build a cross-functional team that includes members from both ABM and vertical marketing. This team should be responsible for developing a unified strategy that leverages the strengths of both approaches.

Step 3: Create Vertical-specific Messaging: With your team in place, the next step is to develop messaging and content that speaks directly to the needs and pain points of your target verticals. This might involve creating case studies, white papers, webinars, and other content that demonstrates your understanding of the industry and your ability to solve its unique challenges.

Step 4: Identify Key Accounts: Once you have your messaging in place, you can start identifying key accounts within each vertical. This might involve using account prioritization models to identify high-potential accounts or working with your sales team to identify accounts that are already engaged with your business.

Step 5: Develop Personalized Campaigns: With your accounts identified, you can start developing personalized campaigns that speak directly to their needs and pain points. This might involve creating customized landing pages, developing targeted email campaigns, or running personalized ad campaigns on social media.

Tactic #37: Integrating Revenue Teams for a 360-Degree ABM Approach

Stage of Funnel: TOFU MOFU

Channels Involved: Martech

Tactic Description: This tactic involves the integration of Customer Relationship Management (CRM) or Customer Data Platform (CDP) with other revenue-generating teams, such as Sales, Marketing, and Customer Success, to create a 360-degree view of customers' businesses and industries. The objective is to collect and analyze multidimensional data about customers, such as their purchasing behavior, preferences, pain points, and industry trends.

Example: A global SaaS company specialized in marketing automation wanted to enhance their customer engagement and revenue generation strategies. To achieve this, they designed an internal platform that integrates their data coming from CRM, CDP, campaigns, social media, web, email and 3rd party subscriptions.

The platform collected and analyzed multidimensional data about its customers and prospects, including purchasing behavior, preferences, customer interactions, product usage, support tickets, customer feedback, pain points, and industry trends. This empowered them to deliver personalized experiences and drive revenue growth.

They employed data analysis and visualization tools to make actionable insights that are comprehensive. By applying advanced analytics, they gained valuable insights into customer behavior, identified patterns and trends, and discovered cross-selling or upselling opportunities.

This data-driven approach helped the teams make informed decisions, personalize their engagement strategies, and deliver targeted marketing campaigns. Armed with a 360-degree view of their customers, the company's Sales, Marketing, and Customer Success teams were better equipped to engage with customers in a meaningful way.

Execution Steps:

1 — Identify the need

Gather inputs from your revenue teams on the data they can capture and the data they want to access. The teams that can be included are Market Research, Communications, Sales, Customer Success, Customer Support and Product team

2 — Hyper Personalize

While deciding on the data fields, keep in mind the data that would be needed to contact, engage, personalize and be more relevant during communication. Also consider the data that would be needed at stages of propensity evaluation, data collecting and tracking the prospect's journey. Determine the teams or individuals who will hold accountability.

3 — Maintain the Data Quality

Keep monitoring the data for discrepancies or even better maintain a dashboard to monitor the discrepancies in real time. You can also reward monthly or quarterly a champ who has captured the data with the best quality.

4 — Grant Access

Once the data capturing model is in place with unification from various teams, you can now look at the aspect of giving the data access to the stakeholders to an appropriate degree based upon their needs.

5 — Keep up with the Martech Changes

As the channels or the tools used across organization keep adding or changing, the data availability changes, accuracy changes, and formats change. This brings the need to have at least a yearly assessment of the data usage across different channels, contexts, and formats that would bespeak the data fields' validity and other data that is missing and should be captured.

Tactic #38: Gamified Data Collection

Stage of Funnel:　　　TOFU　　　　　　　MOFU

Channels Involved:　Event, In-person meet and Martech.

Tactic Description: The objective is to make the data collection process more engaging and fun, resulting in higher response rates and better-quality data.

To execute this tactic, companies can design a game or a series of games that incentivize prospects and customers to share their information. The game could be a quiz, a puzzle, or a scavenger hunt that requires the participants to answer questions related to their business or industry. Companies can also use leaderboards and rewards to motivate participants and make the game more competitive.

Example: A global IT organization has introduced a game to capture information from customers and prospects in a more engaging and collaborative manner. The game underwent initial testing through pilot programs, allowing the organization to refine its rules and gamification process.

The game was designed as a multiplayer experience to encourage collaboration and streamline the process. Every time a participant was asked a question, their input was recorded. However, the unique aspect was that all other participants were also given the opportunity to respond by agreeing or disagreeing with the answer provided. This approach ensured input from various departments of each participant, creating a 360-degree view encompassing multiple customer contexts.

By utilizing this interactive game, the IT organization fostered a collaborative environment where valuable insights and perspectives were shared. This innovative approach enabled the organization to gather comprehensive information from customers and prospects, enhancing their understanding of various customer contexts and facilitating more informed decision-making.

Execution Steps:

Define the Objective

Determine what data you want to collect and how you plan to use it.

Identify the Audience

Determine who your target audience is & what motivates them.

↓

Choose the game Mechanics

Choose the game mechanics: Select game mechanics that will motivate and engage your audience. Examples include leaderboards, badges & rewards.

↓

Develop the game narratives

Create a compelling story that ties the game mechanics to the data you want to collect. This will make the game more engaging and help participants understand the value of their participation.

↓

Test & Iterate

Test the game with a small group of participants and gather feedback. Use this feedback to refine the game and improve engagement.

↓

Analyze the data

Use the data collected through the game to inform your ABM strategy and personalize your outreach to prospects and customers.

Tactic #39: Automating Account Research and Data Capture

Stage of Funnel: TOFU

Channels Involved: Martech

Tactic Description: Establish sources for researching accounts and automate the process of capturing data from those sources. By doing so, you can gain a 360-degree view of your target accounts and their business activities, allowing you to develop more effective account-based marketing strategies.

Example: An application development company implemented a robust strategy to establish reliable sources for researching accounts and automate the process of capturing data. They identified key sources of information that would provide valuable insights into their target accounts. These sources included industry publications, technology forums, social media platforms, business directories, and relevant software development communities. They also explored third-party data providers that specialized in aggregating data on companies and their technology needs.

To automate the data capture process, the application development company leveraged advanced technologies such as web scraping, data mining, RPA and application programming interfaces (APIs). They developed custom software tools and integrated them with their existing customer relationship management (CRM) and marketing automation platforms. These tools were designed to retrieve, organize, and update data from the identified sources automatically.

They have set up web scraping algorithms to extract relevant information from technology blogs and forums. They also utilized APIs to connect with external data providers and pull real-time data on companies, such as their technology stack, recent projects, and hiring trends.

The automated data capture process enabled the application development company to identify triggers and signals that indicated potential opportunities or challenges for their target accounts. For instance, they could track technology acquisitions, funding announcements, or industry events that might impact their prospects' development initiatives.

Overall, this approach allowed them to gather data without human dependency, with more frequency for refreshed data, more accuracy, consistency, saving time and driving a more personalized approach to prospects and customers.

Execution Steps:

Step 1: Identify Key Sources

Start by identifying the most valuable sources of information about your target accounts. These could include annual reports, revenue growth, persona growth, press releases, CRM data, client websites, social media pages, and LinkedIn profiles of key stakeholders.

Step 2: Set up Automation

Once you've identified your sources, set up automated processes for collecting data from them. This could involve using web scraping tools, social listening platforms, or APIs to automatically pull data into your CRM or other marketing systems.

Step 3: Dashboard for Data

To make sense of the data you're collecting, develop dashboards that allow you to analyze it in a way that's easy to understand. This could include visualizations that show trends in data over time or reports that highlight key insights and opportunities.

Tactic #40: Advanced Account Analysis for ABM

Stage of Funnel: TOFU   MOFU   BOFU

Channels Involved: In-person meet and Martech

Tactic Description: The ABM tactic of doing deeper account analysis or evaluation involves conducting various analyses to gain a better understanding of the target account.

Porter Five Force Analysis: This framework focuses on five key forces: the bargaining power of suppliers, the bargaining power of buyers, the threat of new entrants, the threat of substitute products or services, and the intensity of competitive rivalry. Porter's Five Forces analysis provides a structured approach to evaluating market dynamics, identifying potential risks and opportunities, and formulating effective strategies to achieve a sustainable competitive advantage.

PESTEL Analysis: PESTEL stands for Political, Economic, Social, Technological, Environmental, and Legal factors. This analysis involves examining the forces that can shape the industry and influence business operations. Political factors include government policies, regulations, and stability. Economic factors encompass economic indicators, such as inflation, unemployment, and exchange rates. Social factors consider societal trends, cultural norms, and demographics. Technological factors involve advancements in technology that can disrupt or enhance business processes. Environmental factors encompass ecological and environmental concerns. Legal factors involve legislation and legal frameworks that impact the business environment. By conducting a PESTEL analysis, organizations can identify opportunities and threats, anticipate market trends, and align their strategies to navigate and capitalize on external factors effectively.

Deep Sentiment Analysis: This is about analyzing the sentiment expressed in the text towards a particular topic, entity, or brand. It enables organizations to gauge customer perception, understands public opinion, and track sentiment trends over time. By harnessing deep sentiment analysis, businesses can gain valuable insights into customer satisfaction, brand reputation, and product performance.

Semantic Analytics: This technique is used to extract meaning and insights from unstructured data, such as text documents, emails, social media posts, and other textual information. Unlike traditional analytics that focuses on structured data, semantic analytics goes beyond simple keyword matching. It explores the contextual understanding of language. By leveraging natural language processing (NLP) and machine learning algorithms, semantic analytics can identify entities, relationships, and concepts within the text.

Execution Steps: Here are some analysis types to understand an account in depth.

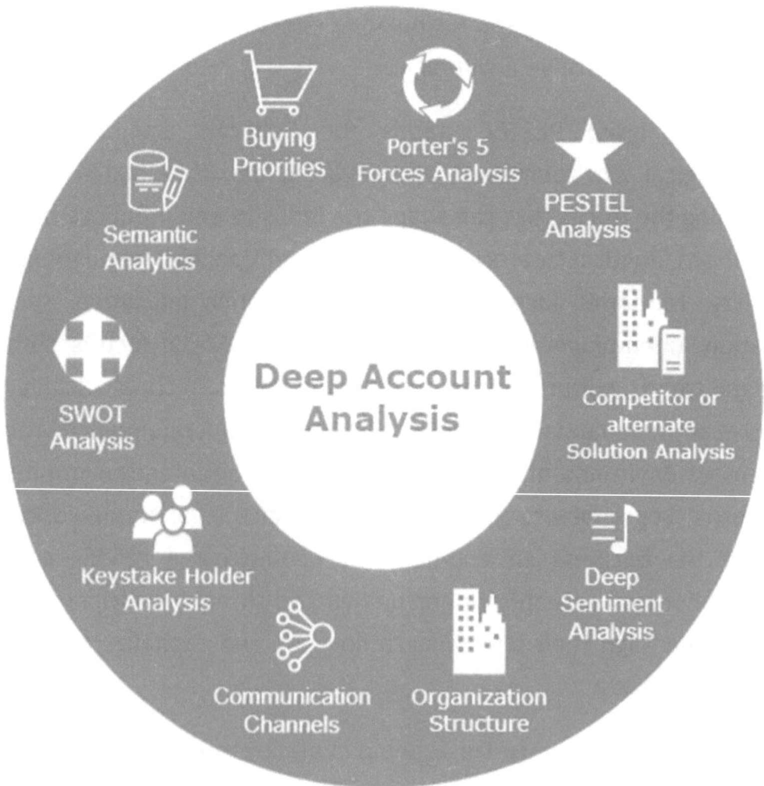

Tactic #41: Establishing a Center of Excellence (CoE)

Stage of Funnel: TOFU   MOFU   BOFU

Channels Involved:

Tactic Description: Developing a centralized function like a CoE (Center of Excellence) for training FSRs (Field Sales Representatives) is a great way to scale up your ABM program without scaling up your ABM team. CoE ensures that your sales team is equipped with the knowledge and skills necessary to effectively execute your ABM program.

Example: A global technology company recognized the need to scale up their Account-Based Marketing (ABM) program to reach a wider customer base and drive revenue growth. However, they wanted to achieve this without increasing the headcount of their ABM team. To accomplish this, they decided to leverage their existing Field Sales Representatives (FSRs) and established a dedicated Center of Excellence (CoE) for ABM.

The CoE, led by the ABM team at the company's headquarters, played a crucial role in training and empowering the FSRs to execute ABM strategies effectively. It was equipped with various resources and capabilities, including policies, budgets, processes, online platform, communities, content assets, training assets, tools, resources, playbooks, integrated techstack, ABM program health checks, and others.

To evaluate the progress of their CoE, they have used metrics such as pipeline, NPS Score, Win rate, Feedback on training sessions, No of FSRs enrolled for sessions, Learning progression of FSRs, Maintenance of CoE,etc. The CoE served as a platform for ongoing learning and improvement. The FSRs could provide feedback, share success stories, and collaborate on refining ABM strategies, ultimately driving continuous improvement in the company's ABM program.

Execution Steps:

Step 1

<u>Define the goals & training curriculum of your COE:</u>

Determine what skills you want your FSRs to have & how you plan to measure success. Develop a training curriculum that will enable your FSRs.

Step 2

<u>Identify training resources:</u>

Identify the training resources that you will use for your COE. This could include training videos, webinars, online courses, focus groups, competitions and in-person training sessions.

Step 3

<u>Assign training coordinator:</u>

Assign a dedicated training coordinator to manage the COE. This individual should be responsible for scheduling training sessions, tracking progress, and ensuring that FSRs have access to the necessary resources.

Step 4

<u>Monitor & evaluate performance:</u>

Monitor & evaluate the performance of your FSRs by tracking sales metrics, customer feedback, and other performance indicators.

Tactic #42: Build Communities Build Your Leadership

Stage of Funnel: TOFU

Channels Involved: Web and Event

Tactic Description: This strategy involves creating a platform or space where your persona audience can share knowledge, experience and ideas related to your product or service. By fostering a community, you can build stronger relationships with your customers & prospects and establish champions who can help advocate for your brand.

Execution Steps:

Step 1 - Identify the right platform

Choose a platform that can best support your community's needs and goals. Consider platforms like LinkedIn Groups, Facebook Groups, Slack channels, or proprietary platforms that offer specialized features for communities.

Step 2 - Recruit members:

Invite customers, users, and partners to join the community and provide value proposition for joining. You can also identify potential champions within your existing customer base.

Step 3 - Provide Relevant Content

Share relevant content that aligns with your customer's interests and goals. Encourage community members to share their own content and experiences as well.

Step 4 - Engage with Members

Actively engage with community members by responding to questions, offering feedback, and participating in discussions.

Step 5 - Foster Networking

Facilitate networking opportunities between community members, such as virtual meetups, webinars, and other events.

Step 6 - Recognize & Reward:

Reward and recognize top-performing members to motivate continued engagement and loyalty.

Tactic #43: Personalized ABM Engagement: Tailoring Outreach to Individual Accounts

Stage of Funnel: TOFU   MOFU   BOFU

Channels Involved: Web, Event, In-person meet, Direct mailer and Email.

Tactic Description:

By using personalization at different levels, marketers can show their target accounts that they are invested in their success and committed to building long-term relationships.

Example: An Edtech company that specializes in educational tools and resources decided to organize a tree-planting CSR (Corporate Social Responsibility) activity as part of their sustainability efforts. They identified an existing customer that has account growth opportunities.

Knowing this was in alignment with the customer's interest, they extended an invitation to co-sponsor the activity without any commercial commitment and share the limelight.

During the tree planting event, the Edtech company ensured an engaging and collaborative experience by providing informative sessions on environmental sustainability and the benefits of trees. They also integrated their educational tools into the activities, incorporating interactive elements to educate participants about the ecosystem and the significance of their efforts.

To maximize the impact and reach of the CSR activity, the Edtech company proactively engaged with the media. They issued a joint press release with the customer, highlighting the event and its objectives. By leveraging their connections with local news outlets and education-focused publications, they secured press coverage for the activity.

The press coverage not only showcased the Edtech company's commitment to sustainability but also highlighted the collaboration between the company and its target accounts. The media coverage created positive brand visibility, strengthened relationships with existing clients and attracted potential clients who shared similar values.

Types of personalization possible:

1: Personalized Welcome Kit

2: Industry trends & Reports

3: Personalized Collaterals

When a new account joins your program, send them a welcome kit that is tailored to their specific industry, challenges, and pain points. This could include case studies, white papers, and other content that is relevant to situation.

Keep up your accounts with the latest trends and reports that are relevant to their industry. This shows that you are invested in their success and are committed to providing value beyond your own products and services.

Create collaterals that are specifically designed for each account. This could include customized product sheets, case studies, & presentations that are tailored to their unique needs or even have their name and logo on the collateral.

4: Personalized Events

Invite key decision-makers at your target accounts to an exclusive executive event.

5: Sponsor CSR Activities

Identify a CSR initiative that is aligned with the values of your target accounts and sponsor it. Invite them to participate and honor their contribution. This shows that you share their values and are committed to make a positive impact.

Tactic #44: Start Small and Grow Big

Stage of Funnel: TOFU

Channels Involved: Channel agnostic

Tactic Description: One of the most frequently asked questions is, how many accounts can I subscribe to the ABM Program? The major factors that decide this are

1.   Stage of the ABM Program,

2.   Martech & Automation,

3.   ABM team and Nature of business, l

4.   ike Business Model, Sales Cycle, ACV, etc.

Example: A Biotech company initiated an Account-Based Marketing (ABM) program by analyzing the genome of the Ideal Customer Profile (ICP) of their top 20% accounts, which contribute over 70% of the company's revenue. They also identified customer accounts with growth potential for further development.

To kickstart the ABM program, they selected 40% of their customer accounts (this depends on how many accounts with growth potential one has) and 60% as greenfield, net new accounts that closely matched their ideal client characteristics. Factors considered were industry, organization size, location, revenue, business model, cultural fit, and geographic footprint.

Strategic ABM was employed for existing customer accounts, while Lite ABM was implemented for greenfield accounts. The company defined an account coverage ratio of 5 to 12, with each Sales Development Representative (SDR) assigned 30 accounts to focus on. Additionally, for every six SDRs, a manager was assigned to oversee the progress of these accounts.

This strategic approach maximized the chances of driving revenue growth and fostering strong customer relationships while expanding into new markets with greenfield accounts.

Execution Steps:

Once the ABM program finds success with its tactics and achieves the expected outcomes, it can then be scaled up in volume to cover more accounts. Scaling too quickly without proper resources can lead to a decrease in the quality of the ABM program.

Tactic #45: Creating Thought Leadership Identity

Stage of Funnel: TOFU   MOFU

Channels Involved: Event and Web

Tactic Description: The idea is to create a unique and memorable identity for your brand that can help in building recognition and credibility among your target accounts. This can be achieved by designing a theme for your roadshows and branding the vehicles with your company's identity.

Similarly, creating a mascot for your brand's thought leadership can help promote your brand's identity and expertise in the industry. These tactics can be useful in building long-term relationships with your target accounts and establishing a strong brand presence in the market.

Example: A SAAS product company utilized an iconic van as a prominent feature in all of its roadshow events. This strategic decision played a crucial role in establishing a strong brand association with creativity, a vibrant culture, and friendliness among the audience.

The van itself was thoughtfully designed, reflecting the company's values of creativity, cultural openness, and a welcoming atmosphere. At certain events, the van served as a visually captivating backdrop, while at others, it was positioned near the event premises, inviting attendees to take selfies with it.

This mascot-like identity proved instrumental in creating a warm and inviting ambiance at the events, fostering an open-minded atmosphere, and leaving a lasting impression on attendees. Moreover, it significantly contributed to brand recollection, reinforcing the company's image as an innovative and approachable entity.

Execution Steps:

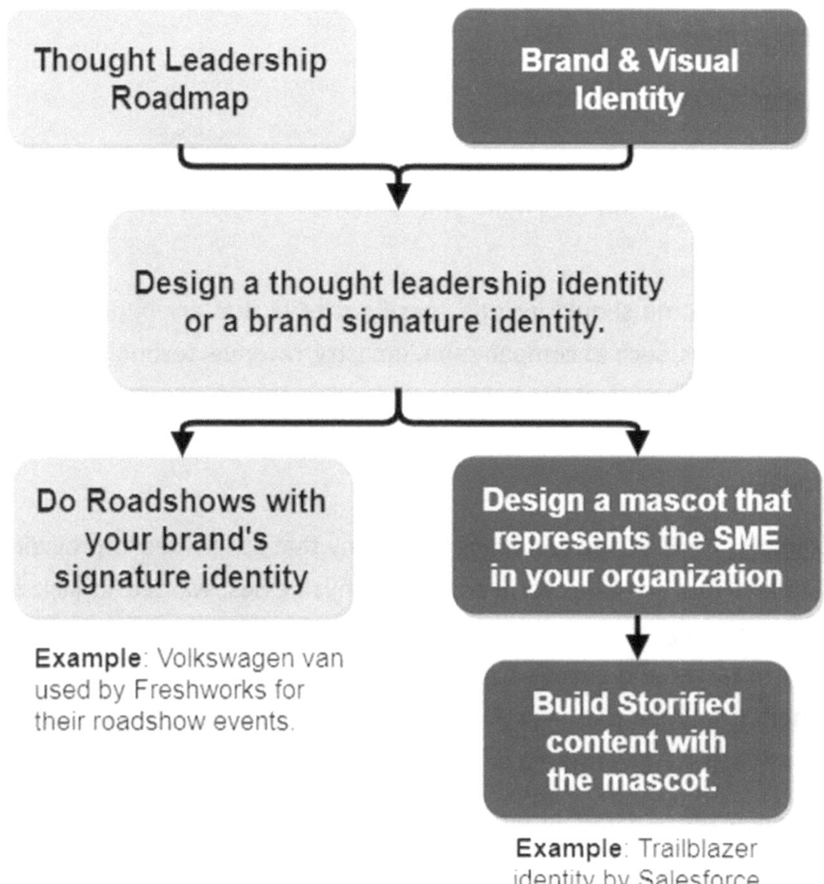

Example: Volkswagen van used by Freshworks for their roadshow events.

Example: Trailblazer identity by Salesforce

<u>Tactic #46:</u> ICP Genome Analysis for ABM.

<u>Stage of Funnel:</u>   TOFU

<u>Channels Involved:</u> Martech

<u>Tactic Description:</u> Designing an ICP genome requires a comprehensive analysis of your top accounts that generate a significant amount of revenue.

The ICP genome should include specific criteria that are important for your business, such as company size, industry, revenue, technology stack, decision-making hierarchy, buying cycle, pain points, and so on. It should be used as a guide to identify and prioritize accounts for your ABM program.

<u>Example:</u> A marketing technology company that specializes in providing data analytics solutions for e-commerce businesses, wanted to kick off their ABM program with the least error margins. Their goal was to leverage ABM to target and engage high-value accounts that were most likely to benefit from their offerings. To achieve this, they recognized the need to define their ICP genome—a detailed profile of their ideal customers.

The company initiated an in-depth analysis of its top accounts, focusing on those that generated a significant amount of revenue. Through this process, they identified specific criteria that were crucial for their business. Some of the criteria were, company size, industry, Technology stack, decision-making hierarchy, pain points, geographical footprints, revenue and YOY revenue growth.

They used the ICP genome as a guide to identify and prioritize accounts for personalized marketing campaigns. They crafted personalized messages that resonated with the prospects and developed content assets that directly addressed the pain points identified in the ICP genome.

Execution Steps:

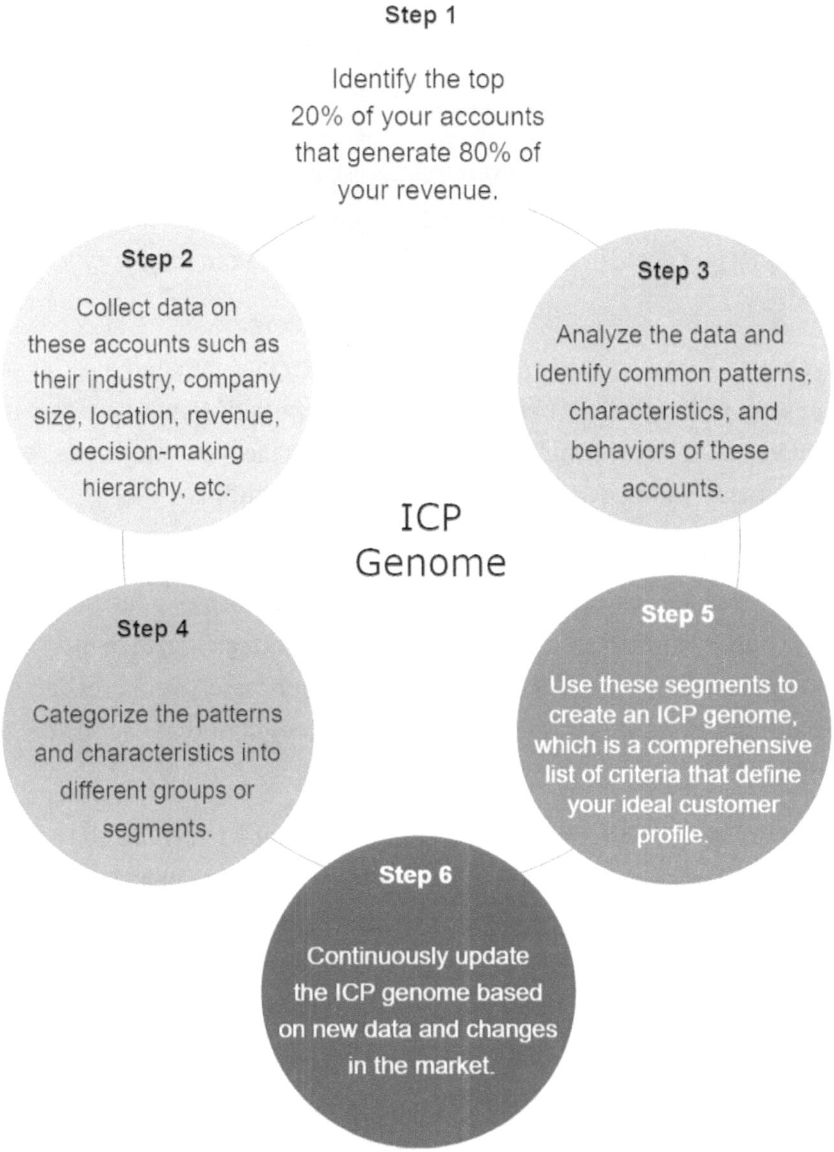

Step 1

Identify the top 20% of your accounts that generate 80% of your revenue.

Step 2

Collect data on these accounts such as their industry, company size, location, revenue, decision-making hierarchy, etc.

Step 3

Analyze the data and identify common patterns, characteristics, and behaviors of these accounts.

ICP Genome

Step 4

Categorize the patterns and characteristics into different groups or segments.

Step 5

Use these segments to create an ICP genome, which is a comprehensive list of criteria that define your ideal customer profile.

Step 6

Continuously update the ICP genome based on new data and changes in the market.

Tactic #47: ABM Perception Interviews for Account Action Planning

Stage of Funnel: MOFU   BOFU

Channels Involved: In-person meet

Tactic Description: Conducting ABM perception interviews is a valuable tactic in ABM. These interviews can help you gain a deeper understanding of your target account's perceptions and needs and can inform your ABM strategy.

Example: A leading marketing automation company initiated a series of in-depth interviews with key stakeholders from their target accounts to gain valuable insights into their perceptions, challenges, and needs. The participants were offered rewards for their contribution.

During the interviews, the company's ABM team probed the participants to understand their current perceptions of the company's offerings, their pain points, and their expectations from a strategic partnership. The interviews also explored the decision-making processes within the target accounts and identified any barriers or misconceptions that needed to be addressed.

The findings from these perception interviews were analyzed and shared with the broader ABM team, allowing them to tailor their messaging, content, and initiatives to align more closely with the target accounts' preferences and requirements. By gaining a deeper understanding of its target accounts' perceptions and needs, the company was able to refine its ABM approach, delivering more personalized and relevant experiences that resonated with its prospects.

This tactic not only enhanced their ABM strategy but also strengthened their overall customer relationships and positioned them as trusted partner in their customers' journey towards success.

Execution Steps:

Step 1

Identify the key decision-makers and stakeholders. Set up one-on-one interviews with these individuals. Design the interview to gather insights and perceptions of your company, business needs, feedback on your product or service, and their culture and purchase process.

Step 2

During these interviews, it's important to listen actively and ask open-ended questions to encourage the interviewee to share their thoughts and ideas. You can also ask targeted questions that will help you understand the metrics or factors they're measuring and how you can align your product or service with their goals.

Step 3

Once you have gathered this information, you can use it to develop an account action plan that is tailored to the specific needs and goals of the target account. This plan should outline specific actions that you can take to address the concerns and needs of the account, as well as opportunities to deepen the relationship and provide

Tactic #48: Blended ABM Approach: Leveraging Different Strategies for Maximum Impact

Stage of Funnel: TOFU

Channels Involved: Martech

Tactic Description: The blended ABM approach is a popular ABM tactic that combines the benefits of different ABM approaches for a more comprehensive and effective strategy. This approach involves using one-to-one, one-to-few, and one-to-many ABM tactics together to cover different tiers of accounts.

By using a blended ABM approach, organizations can cover a wider range of accounts with a mix of highly personalized and more programmatic approaches. This can result in a more efficient use of resources and a more comprehensive ABM strategy.

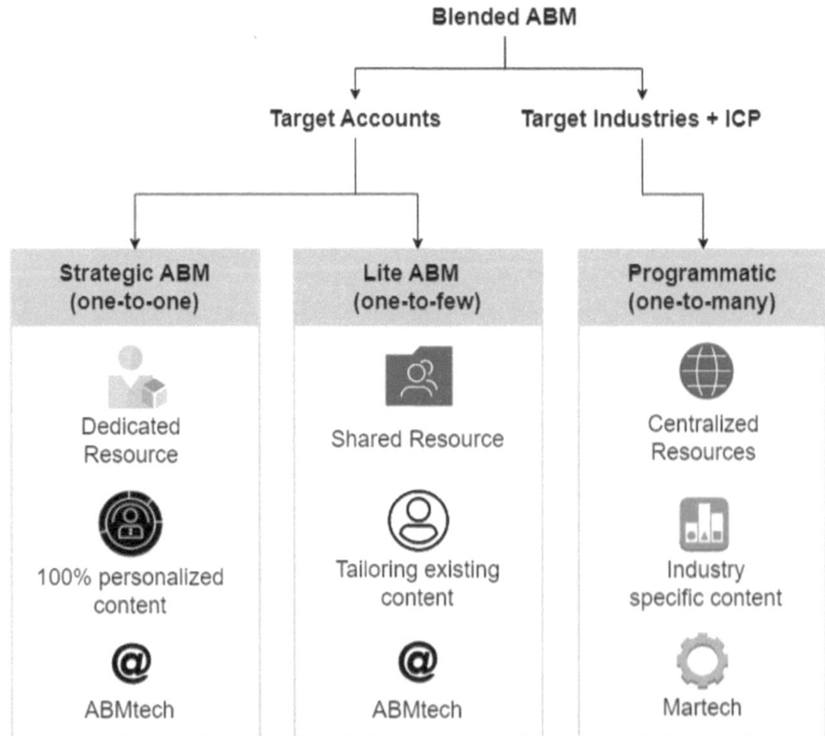

Execution Steps:

Step 1: Identify the strategic accounts that require a one-to-one approach and allocate dedicated resources for each account.

Step 2: Determine the accounts that could benefit from a one-to-few approach, where you can share resources across multiple accounts. These accounts should have some similarities and can be targeted with lite ABM tactics.

Step 3: Determine the accounts that can be targeted with a programmatic one-to-many approach using technology. These accounts should have some similarities and can be targeted with programmatic ads, social media outreach, and other automated ABM tactics.

Step 4: Develop customized messaging and content for each account segment, tailored to their specific needs and preferences.

Step 5: Train and align all sales and marketing teams to ensure everyone understands the different account segments and the tactics being used for each segment.

Step 6: Measure the effectiveness of each approach using KPIs like engagement rates, pipeline contributions, and revenue generated. Adjust your approach as needed to optimize results.

Step 7: Continuously monitor the account segments and adjust your strategy as needed to ensure you are targeting the right accounts with the right approach at the right time.

Tactic #49: Identifying Growth Opportunities in Accounts

Stage of Funnel: BOFU

Channels Involved: In-person meet, Event and Martech.

Tactic Description: Identifying growth opportunities in accounts is an important aspect of ABM, as it helps in maximizing the revenue potential of existing accounts.

On average, it would take 2.5 times to acquire a net new account compared to that of retaining, cross-selling or upselling to the existing account. But unfortunately, many organizations turn a blind eye to the gold mine that exists right under them.

Execution Steps:

Step 1: Conduct a thorough account analysis: Before identifying growth opportunities, it's essential to understand the current status of the account. Conduct a comprehensive account analysis to identify areas of strengths, weaknesses, opportunities, and threats (SWOT analysis), and to determine where the account is in its lifecycle.

Step 2: Identify areas for growth: Once you have a clear understanding of the account's current status, it's time to identify areas for growth. This can be done by analyzing the account's business goals and priorities and identifying areas where your products or services can help them achieve those goals.

Step 3: Determine the potential revenue: Analyze the account's historical data and project future revenue based on the growth opportunities identified. This can determine the potential revenue from specific areas of growth.

Step 4: Develop a growth plan: Outline the steps that need to be taken to capitalize on the growth opportunities, including what products or services to offer, how to position them, and how to communicate with the account.

Step 5: Execute the growth plan: Executing the growth plan involves working closely with the account team to ensure that they understand the plan and are equipped to execute it. It may also involve working with other departments within your organization, such as marketing and sales, to ensure that the plan is communicated effectively and that the necessary resources are allocated to support it.

Step 6: Monitor and measure results: Finally, it's important to monitor and measure the results of the growth plan to ensure that it's working effectively. This may involve tracking key performance indicators (KPIs) and adjusting the plan as needed to ensure that it's delivering the desired results.

Tactic #50: Maximizing ABM Success with Multi-Source Intent Data Analysis

Stage of Funnel: TOFU

Channels Involved: Martech

Tactic Description: Using multiple sources of intent data is a powerful ABM tactic that can help you identify accounts that are in-market and ready to buy. Intent data is information that indicates a company's interest in a particular product or service. By analyzing intent data from various sources, you can gain a more comprehensive understanding of an account's behavior, interests, and intent.

Develop highly targeted campaigns and personalized messaging for each account. This can increase your chances of engaging with accounts that are already interested in your product or service, and ultimately increase conversions and revenue.

Example: A B2B software company employed multiple sources of intent to identify accounts that are actively searching for solutions like theirs. The company subscribed to multiple intent data platforms and also leveraged first hand intent data they gathered from public portals.

Their ABM and sales teams reached these companies with personalized messaging for each account based on the pain point or solution that is reflected in the intent topic. By being more appropriate to the account's needs, they increased their chances of engaging with accounts that are already interested and ready to make a purchase.

Some common sources of intent data include

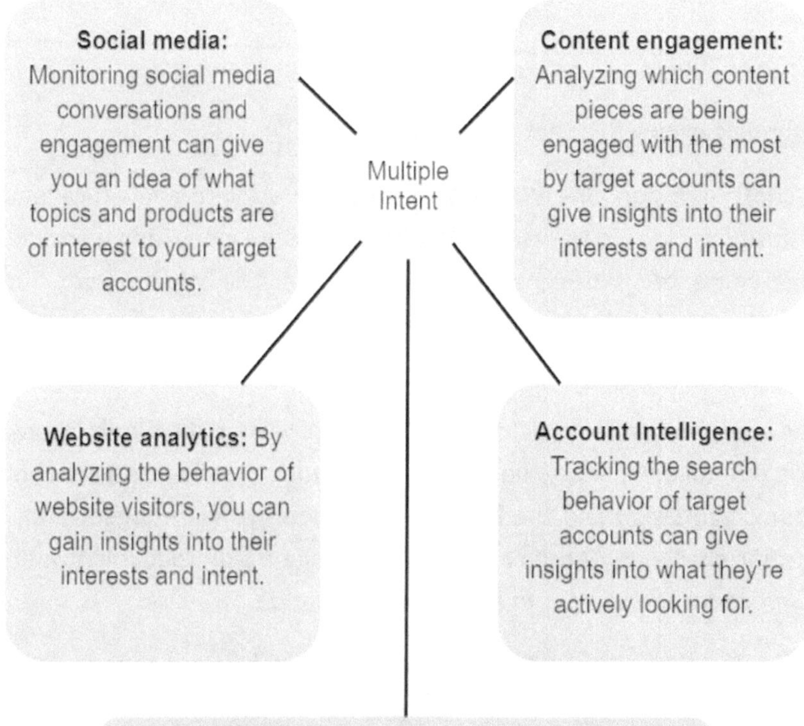

Tactic #51: Innovation Workshop Collaboration with Leading Academic Institutions

Stage of Funnel: MOFU   BOFU

Channels Involved: Event

Tactic Description: One ABM tactic is to collaborate with leading academic institutions, such as Harvard or MIT, to conduct an innovation workshop. This workshop is designed to immerse key stakeholders from both organizations in a business challenge resolution process that encourages ideation, brainstorming, and live demonstrations of proposed solutions.

The workshop can be structured in a variety of ways, but typically involves bringing together cross-functional teams from the client organization, your organization and the academic institution to work together on a specific challenge. These challenges can range from product innovation to process improvement to digital transformation.

Example: A renowned technology consulting firm collaborated with leading academic institutions to conduct an innovation workshop. They partnered with a prestigious university known for its expertise in technology and entrepreneurship to host a two-day workshop focused on digital transformation in the healthcare industry.

The workshop brought together key stakeholders from the consulting firm, client organizations in the healthcare sector, and academic experts from the university. The participants formed cross-functional teams and were tasked with addressing specific challenges related to improving patient outcomes through digital solutions.

Throughout the workshop, participants engaged in collaborative discussions, ideation sessions, and hands-on exercises to develop innovative strategies and solutions. They had access to the university's state-of-the-art research facilities, cutting-edge technologies, and expert guidance from professors and researchers.

The workshop culminated in a presentation session where each team showcased their proposed solutions and demonstrated how they could address the identified challenges. The event provided a platform for knowledge exchange, networking, and fostering partnerships between the consulting firm, client organizations, and the academic institution.

By collaborating with a leading academic institution, the consulting firm demonstrated its commitment to innovation and thought leadership in the healthcare industry. The workshop facilitated the sharing of expertise, generated new ideas, and established valuable connections with key stakeholders.

Execution Steps:

Step 1: Identify the business challenge or problem you want to address in the innovation workshop. Research and identify leading academic institutions with innovation workshops, such as Harvard or MIT.

Step 2: Contact the academic institution and inquire about their innovation workshop offerings, including duration, cost, and workshop format. Select the team members who will attend the workshop, including key decision-makers, subject matter experts, and stakeholders.

Step 3: Collaborate with other workshop participants to generate ideas, approaches, and solutions to the business challenge or problem. Select the best ideas and approaches and develop a plan for implementation.

<u>Tactic #52:</u> Grow as a Trusted Advisor

<u>Stage of Funnel:</u>   BOFU

<u>Channels Involved:</u> In-person meet, Event and PR.

<u>Tactic Description:</u> The goal of this tactic is to build strong relationships with your accounts, establish your credibility and expertise, and position yourself as a trusted partner rather than just a vendor.

By focusing on building strong relationships with your target accounts and providing them with valuable insights and thought leadership, you can position yourself as a trusted advisor and increase the likelihood of winning their business.

Activities to become a trusted advisor:

STEP 1: Meet Regularly

Schedule regular meetings with your accounts, but focus on building relationships and understanding their business goals and challenges. Avoid pitching your products or services at every meeting, instead use this opportunity to learn more about their business and build trust.

STEP 2: Understand their roles and responsibilities:

Take the time to understand the roles and responsibilities of key decision-makers at your target accounts. This will help you tailor your messaging and approach to their specific needs and challenges.

STEP 3: Publish high quality thought leadership

Publish high-quality thought leadership content that addresses the business and industry issues that are important to your target accounts. This can include white papers, blog posts, videos, webinars, and other types of content that demonstrate your expertise and provide value to your accounts.

STEP 4: Hold executive-to-executive networking events

Hold executive-to-executive networking events with local industry peers to help build your credibility and establish yourself as a thought leader in your industry.

Tactic #53: **Cause-Based ABM**

Stage of Funnel: BOFU

Channels Involved: Event

Tactic Description: Cause-based ABM is about understanding the personal interests and values of the decision-makers within an account and finding ways to align your company's initiatives with those interests. By doing this, you can create deeper connections with your prospects and customers, and position your company as a partner who shares their values and goals. Some of the initiatives are on Sustainability, Carbon Neutrality, fundraising, etc.

Example: A technology company specializing in renewable energy solutions implemented the cause-based ABM tactic to establish deeper connections with their target accounts. They recognized that sustainability and environmental consciousness were important values for decision-makers within their key accounts, and they wanted to align their company's initiatives with those interests.

To demonstrate their commitment to sustainability, the company launched a comprehensive carbon neutrality program. They partnered with environmental organizations and experts to conduct a thorough assessment of their carbon footprint and implemented measures to reduce emissions throughout their operations.

In collaboration with its target accounts, the company organized fundraising events and initiatives focused on sustainability. They invited key decision-makers from their accounts to participate in charity runs, tree-planting campaigns, and environmental awareness workshops. These events provided an opportunity for meaningful engagement, networking, and fostering stronger relationships based on shared values.

Additionally, the company developed customized solutions and services specifically designed to help their accounts achieve their sustainability goals. They provided comprehensive energy audits, offered renewable energy solutions, and implemented energy-efficient technologies to help their clients reduce their carbon footprint and operate more sustainably.

They not only demonstrated their commitment to environmental values but also addressed the specific needs and interests of their target accounts. This approach fostered deeper connections, increased customer loyalty, and created a positive brand image associated with sustainability and shared values.

Execution Steps:

Step 1: Identify the key decision-makers within your target accounts. Use LinkedIn, company websites, and other sources to gather information on their professional background and personal interests.

Step 2: Research the causes and initiatives that are important to those decision-makers. Look for information on their social media profiles, personal websites, and other online sources.

Step 3: Identify and plan an event or initiative that showcases your company's alignment with the decision-maker's interests. This could be a fundraising event for a charity, a workshop on a relevant topic, or an initiative that promotes a shared cause.

Step 4: Invite the decision-maker to participate in the event or initiative, and position it as an opportunity to network with like-minded professionals and make a positive impact.

Tactic #54: Free Expert Advice Program by SMEs (Subject Matter Experts)

Stage of Funnel: TOFU

Channels Involved: Event, SEO and Social Media.

Tactic Description: The ABM tactic of offering a free 20-minute consultation with a subject matter expert (SME) can be an effective way to build trust and credibility with potential customers.

Why this tactic plays a major role:

Reason 1: This tactic showcases your expertise and is based on the idea that customers are more likely to do business with a company if they believe that the company is knowledgeable and can offer valuable insights and solutions.

Reason 2: A lot of tech leaders are inclined to talk to someone in technology or a subject matter expert. This could attract more response when CTOs or CIOs or CISOs are your personas.

A free 20-minute consultation with an SME can be an effective ABM tactic for building trust and credibility with potential customers. By demonstrating your expertise and offering valuable insights and solutions, you can differentiate your brand and position yourself as a trusted partner in your customers' success.

Example: A Marketing Automation company has offered a free 20-minute consultation with one of their martech experts to Prospects. They promote this offer through personalized outreach emails, targeted social media ads, and a website.

When a prospect expresses interest in the consultation, along with sharing their company details and existing marketing tech stack, they are connected with a knowledgeable SME who guides them through a personalized session. During the consultation, the SME provides expert advice, offers insights into industry best practices, and addresses specific challenges the prospect is facing in their marketing efforts and how their martech product can help them. This personalized approach demonstrated their commitment to potential prospects.

Execution Steps:

Step 1

Identify your SMEs

Determine who in your organization has the expertise and experience to provide meaningful insights and advice to customers. These individuals should be able to demonstrate a deep understanding of your industry, your products or services, and the challenges your customers are likely to face.

Step 2

Develop Value Proposition

Articulate what customers can expect to gain from a consultation with your SMEs. This might include a better understanding of their business challenges, potential solutions to those challenges, and a roadmap for implementing those solutions.

Step 3

Promote the Program

Use a variety of channels to promote the free consultation program, including email, social media, webinars, and events. Make sure to emphasize the expertise of your SMEs and the value that customers can expect to receive.

Step 4

Streamline & Automate Process

Make the process as easy as possible for customers to sign up for a consultation. Use a simple online form to collect basic information about the customer's business and technology needs, and make sure that your SMEs are available to schedule appointments in a timely manner.

Step 5

Follow Up

After the consultation, follow up with customers to ensure that they received the value they expected and to answer any remaining questions they may have. This can be an opportunity to deepen the relationship and move the customer closer to a sale.

Tactic #55: Thought Leadership Promotional Activities

Stage of Funnel: MOFU   BOFU

Channels Involved: PR, Event and Social Media.

Tactic Description: The ABM tactic of thought leadership promotional activities through participating in interviews or co-authoring content is an effective way to establish credibility and showcase expertise in a particular field. By partnering with credible channels, you can expand your reach and connect with a wider audience.

Execution Steps:

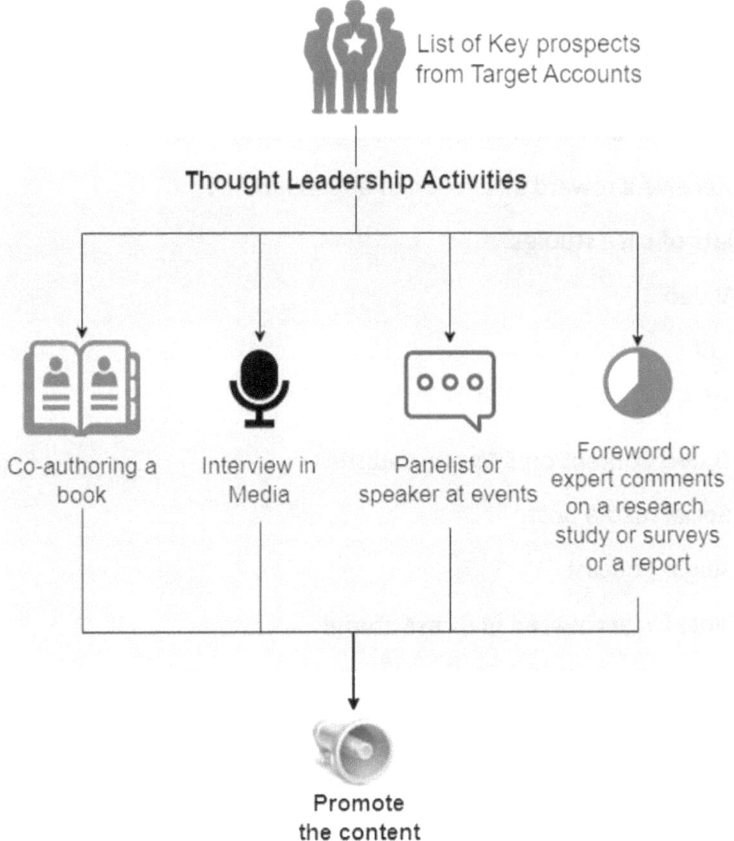

Tactic #56: Build Champions from Your Customers

Stage of Funnel: BOFU

Channels Involved: PR, Events, Social Media and Content Syndication.

Tactic Description: The ABM tactic involves actively seeking customer feedback and encouraging satisfied customers to share their positive experiences and outcomes.

Here are some Value Propositions that you can offer them about contributing to a case study:

1.   Free Advertising and media press releases

2.   Free Organization's brand recollection

3.   Possibility of being nominated for awards

4.   Appreciation boost for internal employees

5.   Personal brand building by voicing the case study

6.   Receive a reward as a token of appreciation.

Formats of case studies:

1.   Video

2.   Pdf

3.   Web page

4.   Gated Content on 3rd party website

5.   Social media post

6.   Audio podcast

Elements to be covered in a case study:

1.   Company name

2.   Company logo

3.   Key stakeholder(s) name(s)

4.   Quotes from the key stakeholder(s)

5.   Videos and photos that can be included in the content

<u>Tactic #57:</u> Employee Briefing and Debriefing for Events

<u>Stage of Funnel:</u>   TOFU

<u>Channels Involved:</u> Event

<u>Tactic Description:</u>

Being prepared for the event in advance can make a lot of difference in the outcome that can be obtained.

<u>Example:</u> A global technology company prepared to participate in a major industry conference where they showcased their latest products and innovations. Before the event, the company conducted thorough internal employee briefings.

They organized dedicated sessions where employees directly involved in the event, such as sales representatives, product managers, and executives, were provided with comprehensive information about the conference objectives, target audience, key messages, and expected outcomes.

During the briefing, employees were encouraged to ask questions, seek clarifications, and provide input to ensure a unified understanding and alignment. They were also equipped with the necessary marketing collateral, product demos, training materials and even reward vouchers to effectively engage with attendees.

After the event, the company conducted debriefing sessions to evaluate the outcomes and gather valuable insights. The debriefing process helped identify areas for improvement, refine future event strategies, and capture valuable customer feedback gathered during the conference.

They updated their internal event playbook, shared best practices, and incorporated feedback into their overall marketing and sales strategies. This resulted in a more cohesive and impactful presence at the conference and enhanced customer interactions and outcomes.

Execution Steps:

Step 1: Identify Your Team

Identify the internal employees who will be participating in the event.

Step 2: Pre-event exercise

Conduct a pre-event briefing session to provide them with relevant information about the event, such as the target accounts being participated in, their research details, and the accounts to be focused on.

Step 3: Empower with insights

Provide them with the areas of interest of the target executives to help them tailor their conversation and engagement accordingly.

Step 4: Gather data

Encourage them to take notes during the event and capture any important data or insights that can be useful for future engagements.

Step 5: Post-event approach

Conduct a post-event debriefing session to document the data that was captured, discuss any key takeaways or learnings, and identify any follow-up actions required.

Step 6: Keep up the momentum

Use the insights and data gathered for the post-event approaches and also inform future ABM activities and refine the approach for future events.

Tactic #58: Build Executive Club

Stage of Funnel: TOFU

Channels Involved: Event, Web, Social Media and PR.

Tactic Description: This is a strategy where you create an exclusive club or community for executives in a particular industry or business segment, with the aim of building relationships, sharing knowledge and promoting your brand as a trusted partner and thought leader.

The key to the success of this tactic is to make the club or community exclusive so that members feel that they are part of an elite group that is privy to unique insights and opportunities. It is important to provide members with tangible benefits such as access to exclusive events, expert speakers, networking opportunities, research reports and thought leadership content.

Example: A leading management consulting firm specializing in the healthcare industry created an exclusive club for healthcare executives. The firm carefully selected a group of high-level executives from prominent healthcare organizations to be part of the exclusive club. Membership was by invitation only, based on the executives' seniority, influence, and expertise within the industry. This exclusivity ensured that members felt they were part of an elite group with access to unique insights, opportunities and experiences.

As part of the club benefits, the consulting firm organized exclusive events, such as executive roundtables, leadership summits and experiential events, where members could engage in strategic discussions, share best practices, and network with their peers. These events featured renowned industry experts and provided valuable insights into the latest trends and challenges in the healthcare sector.

The executive club also facilitated networking opportunities, introductions and provided an online platform for ongoing engagement and knowledge sharing among the club members.

Execution Steps:

Step 1
Define the clusters of your key personas. Choose one of the personas to start building a community for. Example: CEO Club, CFO Club, CTO Club, etc.

Step 2
Design the vision and mission of the groups and the kind of impact you want to bring in. Once the vision and roadmap are ready, register the community.

Step 3
Develop a compelling value proposition for the club or community, highlighting the benefits of membership such as access to exclusive events, expert speakers, networking opportunities, research reports, and thought leadership content.

Step 4
Develop a website and social media presence that can help you connect with potential members and raise awareness about your community. Make sure your website is easy to navigate and provides information about your mission, events, and membership. Keep your brand as subliminal as possible.

Step 5
Develop a team of dedicated volunteers from your persona who share your vision and are willing to help you get the community up and running. Look for people who have skills and expertise that can contribute to the community. You can use your existing contacts or leverage your account-based marketing (ABM) programs to identify key decision-makers and influencers.

Step 6
Hosting events and activities is a great way to bring your community together and create engagement. Consider organizing workshops, webinars, or networking events that are relevant to your field.

Step 7
Building partnerships with other organizations or individuals in your field that complement your product or services. This can also open up possibilities for strategic partnerships. Look for opportunities to collaborate on events or projects.

<u>Tactic #59:</u> Value Addition through Various Content types

<u>Stage of Funnel:</u> TOFU   MOFU   BOFU

<u>Channels Involved:</u> Almost all the channels.

<u>Tactic Description:</u> This tactic talks about contributing through content. There are several contexts of content that can contribute to the experience of your customer or prospect.

Types of Content:

1. This tactic is about creating and sharing

2. educational content,

3. best practices,

4. case studies,

5. tools, templates,

6. FAQs and their solutions,

7. regular recommendations,

8. usage reports,

9. support sessions,

10. product or solution roadmaps,

11. metrics to measure success.

By offering valuable and relevant content, businesses can position themselves as trusted advisors, address customer pain points, and build stronger relationships with their target accounts.

Tactic #60: Celebrate In-Account Day

Stage of Funnel: BOFU

Channels Involved: Event

Tactic Description: The ABM tactic of doing an in-account day is a strategy where a company dedicates a day to spend time with their key account, typically at their office. This day is designed to deepen the relationship with the account and provide an opportunity to gain a deeper understanding of their needs and challenges.

The goals of an in-account day can vary depending on the company's objectives. Some of them are:

1.   Demonstrate new products or services.

2.   Gather feedback on existing offerings.

3.   Build stronger relationships with key decision-makers in the account and establish a better understanding of their organization and its culture.

Example: A software solutions company specializing in enterprise technology implemented an in-account day strategy with one of their key accounts, a leading financial institution.

The company dedicated a specific day to visit the financial institution's office and engage with key stakeholders, including decision-makers, department heads, and end-users. The objectives of the in-account day was to demonstrate new products or services, gather feedback on existing offerings and build stronger relationships.

This personalized approach demonstrated their commitment to the account's success and positioned them as a trusted partner in driving digital transformation within the financial institution.

Execution Steps:

Step 1

Identify their key accounts with account growth opportunities and select the ones that would benefit most from this type of event. Then identify the key decision-makers and stakeholders within the account such as executives, department heads, technical experts, and other employees who can provide value to the account.

Step 2

Develop a tailored agenda with specific objectives and outcomes that aligns with the interests and needs of the target account. This may include a mix of presentations, workshops, celebrations, memento presentations, awarding best users, and interactive sessions.

Step 3

Plan the logistics for the day, such as the date, time, location, and agenda. Send personalized invitations to the key decision-makers and stakeholders within the target account. Develop and communicate the value proposition of the in-account day.

Step 4

On the in-account day, focus on engaging and delivering informative content that addresses the interests and needs of the attendees. Collect feedback from attendees and use it to inform future in-account days or other ABM tactics. Follow up with attendees after the event to continue building relationships and nurturing opportunities.

Tactic #61: In-depth Executives profiling

Stage of Funnel: TOFU

Channels Involved: Martech

Tactic Description: This tactic of conducting detailed research on the prospect involves gathering comprehensive information about them to better understand their needs, preferences, and motivations. This research includes three key components: a basic profile, a buyer persona, and a psychological profile.

By conducting this comprehensive research, ABM practitioners can gain valuable insights into the prospect's background, preferences, and mindset. This information serves as the foundation for crafting personalized messaging, content, and strategies that resonate with the prospect and increase the chances of successful engagement.

Example: An IT services company specializing in cloud computing solutions wanted to engage with a large financial institution as a potential client. To ensure their approach was personalized and effective, they conducted detailed research on the prospect.

The company gathered essential information about the financial institution, such as its size, industry, location and key decision-makers. They studied the institution's technological infrastructure, current IT challenges, and any recent developments in the financial industry.

The company delved deeper into understanding the prospect's buyer persona. They researched the roles and responsibilities of the key decision-makers involved in IT procurement and technology adoption. This included identifying their pain points, goals, and challenges specific to their roles within the institution. By gaining insights into the prospect's buyer persona, the company was able to tailor its messaging and value proposition to address the unique needs and priorities of each decision-maker.

They also researched the prospect's online presence, industry publications, thought leadership content, and public statements.

Execution Steps:

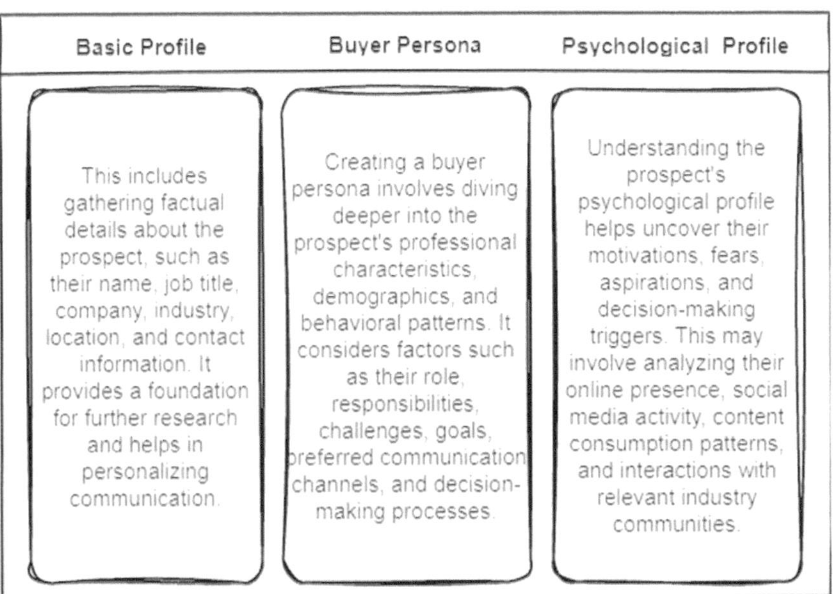

Basic Profile includes: Name, Current job title, previous job roles, social media handles, current company name, industry, sub-industry, revenue, online and offline communities he is part of, contribution interests, awards, achievements, academic qualification, hobbies, interests, family structure, living city, events he participated in, etc.

Buyer Persona includes: their pain points, priorities, processes, opportunities untapped, stage of their journey towards the solution your product or solution is offering, decision criteria, information sources they bank on, buying process, etc.

Psychological Profile includes: the language, the words they are inclined towards, values, favourite personality types, colours, patterns, etc.

6. Challenges of ABM

Despite being such a novel approach and strategy, ABM still has a few challenges. Most of these challenges are stemmed out from the lack of knowledge or expertise in ABM.

Challenge #1. Data Management:

Have a data strategy in place that not only accommodates various data, but also provides data access at the right degree and keep it comprehensive using dashboards.Your account data foundation plays a crucial role here.

Challenge #2. Identify the right accounts:

With the right skills of analyzing the data and revenue potential, strategically align our campaigns. We have to carefully select the best accounts. It's like creating a recipe for success.

Challenge #3. Personalization at scale:

Personalization is a no-compromise zone in ABM. Having proper competitive and account intelligence tools along with comprehensive data framework makes the personalization possible at scale.

Challenge #4. Alignment and Collaboration:

Implementing ABM successfully requires breaking down silos, collaborative revenue teams and even creating a secret language of collaboration. It's like solving a mystery, but the reward is unlocking the full potential of ABM.

Challenge #5. Tailored Content:

Developing tailored content for ABM is like being a master chef, but it requires time, resources, consistency, and the ability to read needs. It's a challenge that promises delicious results if we can get the recipe just right.

Challenge #6. ABM Adoption:

Getting buy-in from key stakeholders can be a challenge.But with persistence and patience, you can design and ABM Program that can break down barriers, unite teams and pave the way for success in the ever-evolving marketing landscape.

Challenge #7. Measuring the ROI:

ABM is a long-term strategy. Measuring its true ROI goes beyond immediate business outcomes. By embracing the journey and adapting measurement strategies, businesses can gain a deeper understanding of the value ABM brings.

www.ingramcontent.com/pod-product-compliance
Lightning Source LLC
Chambersburg PA
CBHW021538150726
47990CB00006B/2297